Revised Edition

Making the Ordinary Extraordinary

Seo Eun-mi

BAEKSAN Publishing Co.

This book was supported by 2010 Howon University Research Grant.

Preface

Preface

"Those who sow in tears shall reap in joy." (Psalm 126:5)

You are in the prime time of your life. You are the jewel of your family and you are a special person. You deserve a wonderful life. Let's make our life extraordinary! Every moment, do your best because you have only one life. Time is gold, and there's no time to waste. You know that you can't buy time.

There's no shortcut to master English. You just need strong determination and diligence if you want to be a fluent English speaker. Just repeat and practice! Remember that practice makes perfect. Your English proficiency will make your life more fun and exciting in this global society.

Good luck!

Seo Eun-mi, Ph.D

Contents

Contents

01 Unit

I was born in the year of the horse.

Ice breaking activity

Let's shake hands with the classmates.

Everybody will line up according to one's birthday and face each other. Shake hands with a partner and introduce yourself briefly. Move to the next person and introduce yourself.

1) Where are you from?

I'm from Seoul, Korea. (I'm not from Jeonju.)

I'm from ____________________.

You're from Busan, Korea. (You're not from Gunsan.)

He's from Tokyo, Japan. (He's not from Bangkok.)

She's from Beijing, China. (Is she from Taiwan?)

They are from Warsaw, Poland.

(Are they from Moscow, Russia?)

We're from San Francisco, USA.

(We're not from Seattle, USA.)

2) When were you born? When and where were you born?

I was born in Seoul

I was born in ______________.

He was born in Kabul, Afghanistan.

She was born in Sydney, Australia.

They were born in Auckland, New Zealand.

We're born in Casablanca, Morocco. (The Kingdom of Morocco)

3) What year were you born according to the Chinese zodiac?

I was born in the year of the horse.

He was born in the year of the pig.

They were born in the year of the dragon.

We were born in the year of the sheep.

(rat, ox, tiger, rabbit, dragon, snake, horse, sheep/goat, monkey, chicken/rooster, dog, pig/boar)

4) When is your birthday?

My birthday is December 16.

Her birthday is ________________.

My birthday is February 14 by the solar (lunar) calender.

I'll be 20 years old in this coming March.

(January, February, March, April, May, June, July, August, September, October, November, December)

5) He's from Brussels, Belgium. People speak Belgian French in Belgium. Belgium is famous for Godiva Chocolatier. (Let's study about a legend of Lady Godiva.)

6) I know someone from Vienna, Austria. I enjoyed espresso in Vienna when I visited there in December, 1995.

7) They're from Johannesburg, South Africa. Johannesburg is the biggest city in South Africa. The capital city is Cape Town. Nelson Mandela was the first South African President (1994–1999). He received the Nobel Peace Prize in 1993. Apartheid was the serious problem in South Africa. Few whites dominated South Africa for a long time. There is still huge gap between the rich and the poor. The whites own more than 80% of the land. The government is trying to solve the serious problems in this country. Everybody is created equal. Apartheid should be abolished in the human society.

8) They came from Dublin, Ireland. The well known writers from Dublin are as follows: James Joyce, George Bernard Shaw, Jonathan Swift, Oscar Wilde, William Butler Yeats etc. Irish musical film *Once* was shot in Dublin. It's a modern day musical about a busker and an immigrant. I like songs from *Once*.

9) Daewon is from Auckland, New Zealand. He immigrated to New Zealand with his family when he was seven years old. He's a perfect bilingual. He'll study culinary arts at the Auckland University of Technology. He wants to be a chef. I'm sure that he'll achieve his dream.

There are two major islands in New Zealand: the North Island and the South Island. The capital city is Wellington. However, the biggest city is Auckland which is called the city of sails. The biggest city in the South Island is Christchurch, the city of garden. A heavy earthquake hit the city of Christchurch in 2011. New Zealanders are also called Kiwi. Kiwi is a bird which cannot fly. Native New Zealanders are called Maori. The best time to visit Auckland is in December which is the summer in New Zealand. Winter is from June to August and summer is December to February.

10) My friend Orawan was born in Bangkok, Thailand. Thailand (The Kingdom of Thailand) is the only Asian country which was not colonized by the other countries. Thais are proud of their history. Most Thais are buddhists.[1] Thai food is hot and spicy. Climate in Thailand is tropical. They have only dry season and rainy season. The first female Prime Minister was elected in July 2011. Her name is Yingluck Shinawatra and she is the younger sister of the former Prime Minister Thaksin Shinawatra.

1) Region: Protestant, Catholic, Buddhist, Atheist

Trip to Thailand (2001, 2008)

I have visited Thailand twice. The first visit was in 2001. I was backpacking with my friend and we stayed at the inexpensive hotels. The second visit was 2008 with my colleagues. We stayed at the five-star hotel in Bangkok. We enjoyed authentic Thai food and Thai massage at the luxurious massage parlor. I tried elephant tracking which was quite unique experience.

The floating market in Bangkok is also famous for tourists. Most people who work in the area of tourism speak good English. There is a famous Kaosan road which is the tourist destination in Bangkok. In this road, we can meet a lot of foreigners from the different countries.

Coconut juice is beautifully decorated with orchid. Coconut juice is great drink to quench your thirst during the scorching hot summer.

Floating market, Bangkok

What happened at "The Bridge on the River Kwai" during World War II?

The Bridge on the River Kwai is a famous movie about the British soldiers in a Japanese prison camp. A unit of British soldiers who were in a Japanese prison camp (western Thailand) worked to construct a bridge over the River Kwai to carry a new railway line.

Citizens in Bangkok take a LRT to commute. Public transportation is convenient and affordable.

Let's study about the capital cities of the other countries. It's important to learn about other countries in this global society. What countries would you like to visit during the vacation?

1. Amsterdam, Netherlands (Holland) - Dutch

2. Athens, Greece: "It's Greek to me." - Greek

3. Berlin, Germany - German

4. Bern, Switzerland - Swiss

5. Cairo, Egypt - Egyptian

6. Jerusalem, Israel - Israeli

7. Kabul, Afghanistan: *Kite Runner* was the first novel written in English by Afghan American. - Afghan

8. Moscow, Russia - Russian

9. Ottawa, Canada: Ottawa is the second largest city in the Province of Ontario. The beautiful province Quebec is French speaking region. Celine Dion is from Quebec. She studied English very hard to become a world-wide singer. Now she is a perfect bilingual. - Canadian

10. Warsaw, Poland - Pole
    What is the name of the well known concentration camp in Poland during the World War II? (Holocaust)

11. Helsinki, Finland - Finnish

12. Oslo, Norway - Norwegian

13. Copenhagen, Denmark - Dane

Trip to Singapore (1993, 2001, 2008)

There are many Indians in Singapore. Several ethnic groups such as Chinese people, Indians and Malays are living in this small country.

This is the Military parade to commemorate the Independence day in Singapore.

I visited Singapore three times: 1993, 2001 and 2008. I have all fun memories spending some time in this small country. There are many towering skyscrapers in Singapore. It is clean and well developed country. When you visit Singapore, you can enjoy Singaporean sling which was a popular alcoholic beverage during the days of British Empire. Singapore is the paradise for shoppers.

People do not sell the chewing gums to keep streets cleaner. The rules are strict and people can be caned if they do not follow the regulations in Singapore. Singaporeans speak good command of English because English is their official language.

Please answer to the following questions

1. Write five things you want to accomplish in this term (semester).

①
②
③
④
⑤

2. What do you think about the Holocaust which means the genocide of six million European Jews during World War II?

3. What is a legend of Lady Godiva? What's the meaning of Peeping Tom?

4. Who are well known writers from Ireland? Who wrote *Gulliver's Travels?*

5. What makes Singapore a wealthy country?

Exercise:

Please fill in the blanks.

Country	Capital city	People
Russia	Moscow	Russian
Israel		
Denmark		
Finland		
Poland		
Afghanistan		
Belgium		
Norway		
Greece		
Switzerland		
Egypt		
Netherlands		

Please write the following sentences in English.

1. 나는 말띠이다.

2. 싱가포르에서는 영어가 공용어이다.

3. 코코넛 주스는 여름에 갈증을 해소하기에 좋은 음료수이다.

4. 태국은 아시아에서 유일하게 다른 나라의 지배를 받지 않은 나라이다.

5. 태국에서 처음으로 여자 수상이 선출되었다.

6. 그들은 남아프리카 공화국의 요하네스버그 출신이다.

7. 남아프리카 공화국에서는 심각한 인종차별 제도가 있었다.

8. 넬슨 만델라는 1993년에 노벨 평화상을 받았다.

9. 우리는 아일랜드의 더블린에서 왔다.

10. 뉴질랜드의 오클랜드를 방문하기에 가장 좋은 시기는 12월이다.

Unit 02

I'm a morning person.

Ice breaking activity: Guessing mimes

Pair work: You'll pair up with your partner. One of you will mime the following sentences. The other person is supposed to guess what your partner is doing.

1) You are opening a tin.
2) You are making a cup of tea.
3) You are watching a comedy on television.
4) You are trying to catch a mosquito.
5) You are reading a very sad story.
6) You are crossing a busy road.
7) You are acting in Shakespeare play.
8) You are waiting for the dentist.
9) You are eating a very hot curry.
10) You are changing a baby's nappy.

(*Grammar Practice Activities*, 2007, p.249)

Grammar: Present progressive

Subject + Be verb + verb..ing

Example: You are opening a can.

He is trying to catch a mosquito.

I'm eating a very hot curry.

They are watching a comedy on television.

1) How many brothers and sisters do you have?

I have one little brother. I have a baby brother.

I have a big brother (big sister).

I don't have any sisters and brothers (siblings).

I'm the baby of the family.

I have one step brother. (step sister)

2) I have one older sister. We are identical twins. She was born 10 minutes earlier than me. We get along pretty well. We major in Early Childhood Education. We'll be kindergarten teachers in the future. We're going to study hard to pass the teacher recruitment examination.

3) Jane is a breadwinner in my family. Paul is a house husband. He takes care of kids and does house chores while Jane is working as a middle school teacher. He'll have a stable job in the near future. Paul thinks being a homemaker is also very important profession.

4) Talking about family

ⓐ I live with my grandparents. My great grandmother passed away six months ago. I'm happy to live with my parents and grandparents. We are the traditional extended family. My uncles and aunts live in nearby.

ⓑ My mother passed away because of cancer. Two years later, my father got married again. Now, I have a step mother and a step sister. Now we are a blended family.

ⓒ I live with my parents and one younger brother. We are a modern nuclear family.

5) My older sister got married two years ago. She visits her in-laws in Lunar New Year and Korean Thanksgiving holidays. My brother-in-law is a family oriented person. He's not a self-centered person. He's willing to help my sister even though he's busy working as a breadwinner. He's a civil servant. My sister delivered fraternal twins (identical twins) last November. I love my niece and nephew. She'll take a leave from work to take care of her children. One year later, she has to find a baby sitter before she goes back to work. It's hard to find a professional baby sitter. Finding a nanny is one of the serious problems for the working mothers.

6) I have a Korean American friend who was adopted by an American couple. She lived in an orphanage before she was adopted. Her American parents gave her good education. She was able to get her BA and MA in English at the Colorado State University. She does not remember her biological parents. She wants to learn about Korean history and culture.

7) When did you graduate from high school?

I graduated from high school in February, 2011.

I graduated from high school in February, 2010. I studied one more year to enter this university.

8) What year are you in?

I'm a freshman.

She's a sophomore.

He's a junior.

We're seniors.

9) Tell us about you.

My first name is Minjee. My first name is ____________.

My family name is Kim. My last name is ____________.

10) What is your major?

It's nursing.

My major is Early Childhood Education.

I major in Business Administration.

My major is ____________.

I major in ____________.

I have double majors.

I minor in ____________.

11) What type of person are you?

I'm a morning person. I try to go to bed a quarter to 11 at night. I like to wake up early in the morning to start my day early. "Early birds catch the worm."

My friend is a night person. She is an night owl. She stays up late, even after the midnight. According to her, she can concentrate better at night.

I'm introverted. I'm shy and timid. When I present in front of my classmates, my mind goes blank. My voice is so small. I have to project my voice so that the audience can listen to what I'm saying. I'm not a people person. On the other hand, my friend is outgoing (extroverted) and she likes to socialize with other people. I like to change my personality. I try to be more optimistic rather than pessimistic.

When you are nervous before your presentation, you can use the following expressions.

* My mind is gone blank.
* I can't think of anything.
* I have some butterflies in my stomach.

Let's make your dream come true!
"Seize the day!" "Make your life extraordinary!"
Let's make our future plans!

What would like to do in the near future?

I would like to be a nurse.

I would like to be a kindergarten teacher.

I would like to be a paramedic.

I would like to be a hotelier.

I would like to be a dental hygienist.

I would like to be an occupational therapist.

I would like to help sick people.

I would like to be a social worker.

I might have my own business.

I would like to teach children at the kindergarten.

I might work at the nursery.

I want to be a professor.

I want to be a flight attendant (cabin crew).

I want to be a military officer.

I want to be a police officer.

I would like to be a fire fighter.

I would like to be an architect.

I want to be a coast guard.

I would like to be a make-up artist.

(beautician, hair-stylist, hairdresser)

I would like to be a fashion designer.

I would like to be a culinary artist (a cook, a chef).

Adult American students are learning Korean as a foreign language (KFL). Learning is a life long education in these days. There are now many foreigners who are trying to learn a Korean language. Can you teach a Korean language to other foreigners?

American society is called a melting pot instead of a salad bowl. There are different ethnic groups in this multi-cultual society. One American student shows his tattoo which is common among America's younger generation. Some say that tattoo can be an expression of an art form.

Exercise:

I. Write the following expressions in English.

1. 나는 우리 집에서 막내이다.

2. 나는 형제, 자매가 없다.

3. 나는 아주 나이 차이가 많이 나는 남동생이 있다.

4. 꿈을 이루어진다.

5. 너의 인생을 특별하게 만들어라!

6. 나는 유치원에서 아이들을 가르치고 싶다.

7. 나는 사회복지사가 되고 싶다.

8. 이번 설날에 나의 언니는 시댁을 방문해야 한다.

9. 나의 한국계 미국인 친구는 입양되었다.

10. 나는 아침 형 인간이다.

11. 나의 언니와 나는 일란성 쌍둥이이다.

12. 나의 형부는 공무원이다.

13. 그녀는 치위생사가 되기를 원한다.

14. 그는 작업치료가 되고 싶어 한다.

15. 우리는 비행기 승무원이 되고 싶다.

II. Please write about your dreams in the future. What do you have to do to achieve your dreams?

III. Please answer to the following questions in English.

1. How many brothers and sisters do you have?

2. Who's a breadwinner in your family?

3. Are you from nuclear family or extended family?

4. What do you think about Korean orphans who were adopted by the foreign parents?

5. When did you graduate from high school? Did you repeat one more year to enter this university?

6. What's your major? Do you have a minor?

7. What type of person are you? (morning person, night person)

8. American society is called a melting pot. Do you know why?

9. What are the effective ways to promote Korean language and culture to the foreigners?

10. When are you going to graduate from university?

When you arrive in America, you have to submit the following form before you go through Customs and Immigration at the airport. Let's practice to fill in this form.

* Family Name: ______________________________
* First Name: ______________________________
* Date of Birth: ______________________________
* Country of Citizenship: ______________________________
* Sex (Male or Female): ______________________________
* Passport Number: ______________________________
* Airline and Flight Number (if applicable): ______________________________
* Country Where You Live – Lawful Permanent Residence: __________
* City Where You Boarded (if applicable): ______________________________
* City Where Visa was Issued (if applicable): ______________________________
* Date Issued (Day/Mo/Yr) (if applicable): ______________________________
* Address While in the United States (Number and Street)
* City and State: ______________________________

03

Unit

How many classes do you have today?

Ice breaking activity:

To do this activity, you have to push the button with your hands and legs. Eventually, you will move all your body parts. Let's have a fun!

My name is Jo. I work at the button factory. One day, my boss came to me and asked "Are you busy?" "No."

"Come here and press this button with you right hand like this."

"Press this button with your left hand like this."

"Press this button with your right foot like this."

"Press this button with your left foot like this."

"Press this button with your forehead like this."

Situation 1

A: I would like to study in the English speaking countries such as the United States or Canada. How can I apply for the graduate school in America?

B: Well, you have to take TOFEL (Test of English as a Foreign Language). You have to study hard to get high score in TOEFL.

A: Studying in the foreign countries is one of my dreams in my life. Even though it's challenging, I want to experience and explore something new in the other countries.

B: You can do it as long as you are determined. Go for it!

Situation 2

A: How many classes do you have today?

B: I have three.

A: Do you have time for lunch?

B: No, I don't.

A: I have four consecutive hours today. I have a kind of hectic schedule. I may grab some sandwich between classes.

B: Don't forget to eat your lunch before you go to class.

Situation 3

A: Do you like your English classes?

B: Yes, I do. It's two credit subject.

A: Who is your professor?

B: My English professor is Dr. Kim (Professor Kim). I like her because she is passionate and enthusiastic. She really cares for students.

A: How many hours do you study English per day?

B: I make it a rule to study English at least one hour every day.

A: Can you tell me the best way to improve English?

B: There's no short cut to study English. You need to practice English every day. "Practice makes perfect."

Situation 4

A: Where are you going?

B: I have to meet my professor in his office. I have a conference with my professor.

A: Where is your professor's office?

B: It is in Building 2.

A: Which floor?

B: It's on the first floor.

Situation 5

A: How many elective subjects are you studying this semester?

B: I have four.

A: Do you have any compulsory (required) subjects?

B: Yes, I have five.

A: What degree are you going to get when you graduate?

B: I'll get a BA (Bachelor of Arts) in Tourism in two years.

A: What about you?

B: I'll get a BS (Bachelor of Science) in Engineering next year. I'm planning to go to graduate school to get an MA (Master of Arts) like my elder brother. He's studying in America now and working on his thesis to get an MBA (Master of Business Administration).

> "I have a dream that my four little children will one day live in a nation where they will not be judged by the color of their skin but by the content of their character."
>
> Martin Luther King

Please match the phrases and places. Where did you hear that particular phrases?

	Phrases		Places
1	Turn to page 109.	a	restaurant
2	Don't feed the bears.	b	bar
3	Single or double dip?	c	classroom
4	A double, on the rocks.	d	donut shop
5	Want me to fill her up?	e	bowling alley
6	Lights! Camera! Action!	f	photo shop
7	Is that for one night or two?	g	hotel
8	Our Sunday Brunch is $9.95.	h	department store
9	Take four of these, twice a day.	i	gas station
10	What size prints do you want?	j	farm
11	Quiet, please. People are reading.	k	New York tour bus
12	Would you like this gift-wrapped?	l	ice-cream shop
13	This should take about a week by air.	m	zoo
14	May I see your boarding pass, please?	n	library
15	Occasional showers throughout the day.	o	bank
16	Let's see, you want a dozen cream-filled?	p	doctor's office
17	Would you like to open a savings account?	q	weather report
18	The wheat will be ready for harvest this week.	r	post office
19	On your left you can see the Statue of Liberty.	s	movie studio
20	Wow! I don't believe it. Two strikes and a spare.	t	airport

(*Ready-made English*, North Star Publishing Company, 1995)

Exercise:

Write down the following expressions in English.

1. 나는 문학사 학위를 받을 것이다.

2. 나의 사촌은 경영학 석사 학위를 가지고 있다.

3. 나의 언니는 미국에서 경영학 석사과정에서 공부하고 있는데, 지금은 석사 논문을 쓰고 있다.

4. 나는 교수님과 면담을 해야 해.

5. 이번 학기에 몇 개의 선택과목을 수강하고 있니?

6. 오늘 수업이 몇 시간 있니?

7. 점심 먹을 시간이 있니?

Talking about scholarship

Situation 1

A: Did you get a scholarship?

B: Yes, I got a scholarship for this semester. I was the second from the top in my department. I got just a partial scholarship this semester.

A: I am so jealous. I admire your strong determination and diligence in studying.

B: Well, you can do it if you are motivated to study.

A: Ok, next semester, I will study hard to get a full scholarship.

B: I'm always number 2 in my department.
My friend Suji is always number 1 in my department.

A: However, I think you have a good leadership. You are the student representative in our department. (You represent our classmates).

"Yesterday is the past."
"Tomorrow is the future."
"Today is a gift, that's why it's called the present."

Situation 2

A: Are you free now?

B: Let's have some coffee and snacks at the English cafe.
They serve excellent quality coffee.

A: Where is the English cafe?

B: It's in the female dormitory. Native speakers are there so we can practice English. They are willing to help you to improve your English.

A: What would you like to drink?

B: Black coffee, please.
I like cafe mocca.
I like caramel machiato.

The first (spring) semester begins in March in Korea. The new school year begins in March. The second (fall) semester starts around the fourth week of August or the first week of September. Some universities offer summer or winter school. Students who want to graduate early like to take classes during the summer.

Group work project: Let's make a video.

They are Americans who are learning Korean language. They made a video using basic Korean expressions. (www.youtube.com: Korean Video Project 2010). Try to make a video with your classmates about your life at campus and share it with the other classmates. It'll be a wonderful memory which you can remember long time.

Living at the dormitory

A: Do you live in the dormitory?

B: Yes, I do. There are two bunk beds in my dorm room.

A: How long does it take from the dormitory to the classroom?

B: It takes at least 10 minutes.

A: Do you have any roommates?

B: Yes, I have two roommates.
We are good friends. We get along pretty well.

A: Can you cook at the dorm?

B: No, we cannot use any electrical devices for security reasons. However, we can use a microwave oven in the corridor in each floor.

A: Where do you eat your meals? Do you have any meal plans?

B: We eat in the cafeteria.
It's a good place to make new friends.

A: Is there any curfew?

B: Yes, we should be back to the dorm at least by 11 o'clock at night.

Living alone

I have to take care of room and board by myself. I don't live in a dormitory. I want my privacy. I don't want to share a room with a friend. I live in a studio apartment in the campus town. My landlord (landlady) is friendly and caring. I'm a tenant. I have to pay the rent at the end of the month. I also have to pay ₩300,000 deposit in advance.

Please write the following expressions in English.

1. 나는 지난 학기에 우리 학과에서 2등이었다.

2. 나는 전액장학금을 받지 못했다.

3. 너는 훌륭한 지도력을 가지고 있다.

4. 나는 기숙사에서 살고 있다.

5. 기숙사의 각 층마다 전자레인지가 있다.

6. 한국에서는 1학기가 3월에 시작한다.

7. 조기 졸업을 원하는 학생들은 여름학기에 공부할 수 있다.

8. 우리 방에는 두 개의 2층 침대가 있다.

9. 나는 세입자이다.

10. 나는 미리 보증금 30만원을 내야 한다.

Festival Week (한국 대학의 축제)

Carrie: Would you please explain about the many festivals which are held on the Korean college campuses? How do you like them?

Jiwon: Well, May is the festival time on Korean college campuses. During the festivals, Korean college students put up many booths and they sell traditional Korean dishes and alcoholic beverages or drinks. They sell this food just for the fun of it.

Carrie: Who cooks the food?

Jiwon: Students volunteer to cook various Korean dishes such as Kimchi pancakes or the traditional Korean barbecue. Kimchi pancakes are popular even though they're a little hot and spicy. It's fun to eat at many of the booths while enjoying entertainment and various activities.

Carrie: As a foreigner, I'm excited about experiencing the Korean college campus festivals. What kind of programs do they have?

Jiwon: There are a variety of programs prepared for students. They sometimes invite famous entertainers. It's a good time to meet entertainers whom they often watch on the T.V. At many of the booths, students hang-up toilet paper and use it as napkins. It's convenient for students to use. It can be very shocking for the foreigners. However, when in Rome do as the Romans do.

Reading

Commencement

In America, Commencement ceremony is held in May since the school year ends in May. In Korea, the college gradation season is in February. Commencement means beginning. Graduation is not the end but it is the beginning of the new chapter of life. College graduates will work in the various fields. They'll learn how to survive in the real world.

Faculty participating in Commencement should wear academic regalia. (2011 Commencement, University of Maryland University College Asia)

I'm the class of 2010. (I graduated from the university in 2010 in America.). In Korea, the class of 2010 means that someone entered the university in 2010. I'm the class of 2011.

Some Westerners are named after biblical names. Those are the common first names. Can you recognize familiar names?

	Biblical names		Biblical names
1	Aaron	21	Mark
2	Abraham	22	Mary
3	Adam	23	Matthew
4	Andrew	24	Michael
5	Benjamin	25	Miriam
6	Daniel	26	Naomi
7	David (King)	27	Nathan
8	Deborah	28	Noah
9	Esther (Queen of Persia)	29	Paul (Apostle)
10	Hannah (Mother of Samuel)	30	Peter
11	Isaiah	31	Philip
12	Isaac	32	Rachel
13	Jacob	33	Rebecca
14	James	34	Ruth
15	John	35	Sarah
16	Jonathan	36	Simon
17	Joel	37	Solomon (King)
18	Joseph	38	Stephen
19	Joshua	39	Thomas
20	Jude	40	Timothy

I. Please write the following names in English.

1. 아브라함
2. 아담
3. 에스더
4. 사라
5. 요셉
6. 리베카
7. 사무엘
8. 솔로몬
9. 다윗
10. 바울

04 Unit

I need to see a dentist.

Ice breaking activity:

Please give three compliments to your partner. Try to find positive expressions. For example:

"You look cool today."

"I admire your passion for learning."

"You are so generous."

"You are so fashionable."

"I like your hair style."

"I like your outfit."

1) Do you know any plastic surgeon? Many women visit plastic surgeon to consult face lifting or plastic surgery. Some Koreans want to have double eyelid surgery. They want to make their eyes big like westerners. Some college students want to have a plastic surgery during the vacation.

2) One of my friends is a medical student. He wants to be a plastic surgeon. My cousin will be a physician and his brother wants to be a dentist.

3) If you have some skin problems, you have to visit dermatologist.

4) Medical insurance in America is expensive. Consultation fee is also expensive.

5) Over the counter medicine: You can buy some medicine over the counter without doctor's prescription. For example, you can buy cough drops or vitamins without doctor's prescription. I used to buy cough drops over the counter when I was in America. Sometimes, we can ask advice from pharmacist over the counter.

6) My sister-in-law is pregnant. The due will be in three months. She is going to deliver a baby soon. She often feels morning sickness.

7) I need to see a dentist. (Dental clinic)
I need to get cleaned my teeth at the Dental clinic.
I have some cavities.
Do you floss after you eat?
Do you carry dental floss with you?
I need to brush my teeth. I also use interdental brush.
I'm really careful regarding dental hygiene.

Please read the following advertisement about the dental clinic. What services can you get in this particular dental clinic?

What we offer:

* Cosmetic dentistry (Veneers, All Ceramic, 1 Hour Tooth Whitening)
* General dentistry (Fillings, Crowns & Bridges, Root Canal, Cleaning, Wisdom Tooth Extraction)
* Implant Dentistry (Single & multiple implants, Overdentures)
* Pediatric Dentistry (Cavity Treatment)

(*Crimson Sky*, July 15, 2011)

8) My elder sister miscarried a baby. She does not take any birth control pills these days. She really wants to have a baby. I feel sorry for her.

9) My mother had pancreatic cancer. She was in ICU=intensive care unit after she got an operation.

10) She was struck with leukemia (cancer of the blood cells).

Useful expressions

* I'm in my period. I need to buy some sanitary napkins.
* People are suffering from diabetes.
* Obesity is a serious problem in America.

Talking about medical symptoms and medication.

1) I have a backache.
2) I have a stomachache.
3) I have a toothache.
4) I have the flu. You have to drink a lot of water.
5) I have a sore throat.
6) I'm coughing hard. I have to take some cough drops.
7) I have been sneezing a lot this morning. You have to cover your mouth when you sneeze or cough. Americans say "Bless you" when somebody sneezes. On the other hand, Koreans don't say anything.
8) I have a runny nose. I need to blow my nose.
9) I have a fever.
10) I have an insomnia. I can't sleep at all. I have to take some sleeping pills.
11) I have an earache.
12) I have a black eye. I have sore eyes.
13) I sprained my ankle.
    I broke my leg. I have to wear a (plaster) cast for two weeks.
    I like to see an oriental medical doctor. Acupuncture is effective to relieve pain.
14) I need some painkiller. I cannot stand the pain.
15) Don't forget to take vitamins everyday.
16) She had a consultation with a psychiatrist (shrink). psychiatric clinic
17) Some people abuse antibiotics.
18) He got an intravenous injection.
19) I'm exhausted.
20) I feel awful. I feel miserable.

Exercise:

Please write the following expressions in English.

1. 나는 링거를 맞았다.

2. 나는 진통제를 사야 한다.

3. 어떤 사람들은 항생제를 남용한다.

4. 나는 발목을 삐었다.

5. 침을 맞는 것은 고통을 완화시키는 데 도움이 된다.

6. 나는 기침을 심하게 한다.

7. 나는 불면증이 있다.

8. 수면제를 먹어야 한다.

9. 나는 몇 개의 충치가 있다.

10. 그녀는 정신과 의사와 상담했다.

11. 그녀는 백혈병에 걸렸다.

12. 그녀는 수술 후에 중환자실에 있었다.

13. 나의 새언니는 임신했다.

14. 그는 성형외과 의사가 되기를 원한다.

15. 나는 치아 관리에 많은 주의를 기울인다.

16. 나는 오늘 아침에 재채기를 많이 했다.

17. 나는 눈에 멍이 들었다.

18. 그는 내과의사이다.

19. 어떤 사람들은 쌍꺼풀 수술을 하고 싶어 한다.

20. 나는 피부과 의사를 방문해야 한다.

Useful expressions

1. Velcro fastener: Velcro is a brand name of hook-and-loop fastener which is used in clothes, shoes to fasten. I like my shoes with velcro fastener.

2. Styrofoam: Styrofoam products such as plates and cups are convenient but they can be harmful for environment. (Green house effect)

3. Battery: My phone is almost out of battery power. (My phone is out of juice.) I need to recharge my phone. Several times, my phone died when my friend called me emergency.

4. Nail clipper: I need a nail clipper to cut my finger nails and toenails. I always carry a nail clipper.

Nail polish: I have to remove my nail polish.
Are there any nail polish in brighter colors?

Pedicure: "I get a facial, a manicure, a pedicure and a massage."
He's an excellent masseur. My masseuse is well trained.

5. CEO: Chief Executive Officer (COO: Chief Operating Officer)

6. CFO: Chief Finance Officer

7. Twist tie: When do you use twist tie?

8. Power strip: We have to use power strip to save electricity.

9. Port-O-let : portable toilet, mobile toilet

10. Kiss and cry zone
It is a place at the stadium where skaters wait for the scores after the performance. It was the name of the TV program of figure skater Kim Yun-a.

What kinds of problems do people have? You can consult about your problems.

Ask Laskas

My daughter, a tenth grader, weighs less than 100 pounds. Her classmates' teasing about her size-"Go eat a hamburger" or "Put some meat on those bones" troubles her. What can I do to comfort her? Is there anything she or I can say to these kids who pick on her?

Petite and Proud

Dear Mother Petite,

Give her context. Let her know that every one of those kids who picks on her has some insecurity about something-frizzy hair, camel lips, caterpillar eyebrows. This is called Being a Teenager. Those years are all about fitting in, and not many teens feel they do. Sadly, one of the lesser laws of human nature is that putting others down makes us feel better (temporarily). Tell her the good news. This stage passes. Let her know that she's beautiful the way she is.

(*Reader's Digest*, April 2011, p.88)

1. What are the problems being out of shape?
2. Why did the classmates tease her daughter?
3. What are the problems of teenagers?
4. What kinds of behaviors do the insecure teenagers have?
5. What is the councilor's advice regarding the problem?

Write down your plans and resolutions in each month. It's important to write down your plans so that you can always remember what you are supposed to do. Don't procrastinate your plans. It's not a good habit to put off things. In each month, try to achieve something special.

January New Year's resolution	February	March
April	May	June
July	August	September
October	November	December

05

Unit

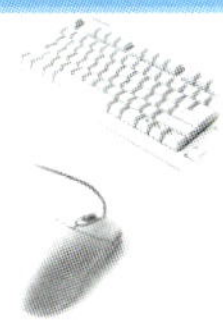

Activities on campus

Ice breaking activity: Hand, clapping activity

Who took the cookie from the cookie jar?

Who me?

Yes you.

Not me.

Then who?

Minji took the cookie from the cookie jar?

We can learn lessons through proverbs.

Actions speak louder than words.

Art is long and life is short.

A barking dog never bites.

Better safe than sorry.

A bird in the hand is worth two in the bush.

Boys will be boys.

Curiosity killed the cat.

Every cloud has a silver lining.

Don't count your chickens before they are hatched.

Don't cry over spilt milk.

Don't put all your eggs in one basket.

The grass is always greener on the other side of the fence.

A hungry man is an angry man.

The leopard does not change its spots.

Don't cross bridges until you get to them.

It's never too late to learn.

You cannot have your cake and eat it.

(*Games for language learning*, Cambridge University Press, 2007 p.89)

Activities on campus

1) Would you like to join our club?
There are many different student club activities around the campus.
It's a wonderful way to make new friends and to get new experience.

2) Students council members are campaigning now.
We will vote for student council members next week.
They work for the welfare of the students.

3) Festival week is in May. Sports week is in October.
Excursion week (MT) is in March. We'll make an excursion to Daechun Beach. Foreigners enjoy mud bath or mud wrestling in Daechun beach in summer time.

4) Field trip: I went on a school field trip to Jeju Island when I was a senior at college. That's my first trip to Jeju Island which is called as Hawaii in Korea. It was exciting five day trip to Jeju Island. We took a ferry from Mokpo to Jeju.

5) Please introduce your school.
I would like to introduce our school. There are around 5,000 students in our university. My university was founded in 1977. There are different majors and disciplines to help students.

Who is the President in your university?

Who is the Dean of Academic Affairs?

Who is the Dean of Student Affairs?

Dr. Kim is a Chair of our Department. Miss Kim is the secretary in our department.

There are many faculty members in our university.

Staff help students in the campus.

6) Let's talk about school facilities.

A: Where is the auditorium?

B: If you go to the Building 5, there is an auditorium in the fifth floor.

A: Is there any fitness room on campus?

B: There's a fitness room at the gym where students can work out.

A: Where is a driving range?

B: It's in front of the big stadium. Students can learn how to play golf at the driving range.

A: Wow! I would like to learn how to play golf.

B: Let's go the driving range. The professional golfer will teach us.

7) Do you like to drive when you commute? What kind of passenger car would you like to drive? I like a compact car instead of a medium-sized car. Name of passenger cars in Korea are as follows. Can you think of other names of passenger cars in Korea?

Genesis	Grandeur	Chairman
Carnival	Galloper	Morning

Activity:

Milling around and find someone who..... Try to talk with at least ten classmates. Write down your classmate's name in each question.

1) Have you ever been to the foreign countries? ______________
   If yes, what country did you go?
   If not, what country would like to visit?

2) Do you like seafood? __________________
   If yes, what kind of seafood do you like?

3) Do you wear undergarments during the winter? ____________
   If not, why don't you wear undergarments during the winter?
   (thermal underwear)

4) Are you a good swimmer? ___________
   If yes, when did you learn how to swim?
   Do you like to swim in the indoor (outdoor) swimming pool?
   You need swimming suit, goggles and swimming cap.
   (breast stroke, back stroke, butterfly style, free style)

5) Do you have a boy (girl) friend)? _____________
   If yes, when and where did you meet your boy (girl) friend?

6) Do you exercise at least three times a week? _____________
   If yes, what kind of exercise do you do?
   Do you lift weights?
   Do you workout?

7) Do you have a driver's license? __________

If yes, when did you get your driver's license?

If not, when do you plan to get your driver's license?

("Phone use while operating a vehicle is prohibited.")

8) Have you tried mud wrestling or mud bath in Daechun? __________

If not, what activity activity do you want to do?

9) Did you join the club on campus? __________

If yes, what club did you join?

If not, what kind of club do you like to join?

10) Do you have an insomnia? __________

I visited Beijing in August 2007.

Let's sing and study English!

1. Do Re Mi Song (From the movie *The Sound of Music*)

Let's start at the very beginning
A very good place to start.
When you read, you begin with A B C
When you sing, you begin with Do Re Mi
The three first notes just happen to be
Do Re Mi
Do Re Mi
Do Re Mi Fa So La Ti
Let's see if I can make it easier.

Doe, a deer, a female deer
Ray, a drop of golden sun
Me, a name I call myself
Far, a long, long way to run
Sew, a needle pulling thread
La, a note to follow sew
Tea, I drink with jam and bread
That will bring us back to Doe, oh, oh, oh

When you know the notes to sing
You can sing most anything.

Exercise:

I. Please write the following expressions in English.

1. 예술은 길고, 인생은 짧다.

2. 짖는 개는 결코 물지 않는다.

3. 계란이 부화하기 전에 계란의 수를 세지 말라.

4. 엎질러진 우유를 보고 울어 보았자 소용없다.

5. 배가 고픈 사람은 화가 난 사람이다.

II. Write down the following expressions in English.

1. 강당
2. 골프연습장
3. 휘트니스 센터
4. 학교 시설
5. 현장학습

III. Let's practice writing. The more you write, the better you can write.

1. Please introduce your school.

2. Please write the most memorable experience in your life.

3. Please write about your role model in your life. Who inspired you to be a better person?

4. Please choose one famous speech and try to deliver that speech. (Martin Luther King, Abraham Lincoln, John F. Kennedy)

06
Unit

Do you workout?

Ice breaking activity: Miming

This is a pair work. Work with your partner.

You are about to / going to

1. You are going to drive a car.
2. You are going to wash your face.
3. You are going to drink a cup of tea.
4. You are going to swim.
5. You are going to play a guitar.
6. You are going to shout.
7. You are going to fall asleep.
8. You are going to work.
9. You are going to pick a flower.
10. You are going to dance.

(*Grammar Practice Activities*, 2007, p.111)

Let's study grammar.

be going to + verb = be about to + verb

Situation 1:

A: Do you exercise regularly?

B: Yes, I do. I exercise almost everyday. How about you?

A: I don't have time to exercise.

B: You need to exercise at least three times a week to be healthy.

A: I just take a walk.

B: Well, I think brisk walking is a good exercise. You can burn off few calories.

A: I really like to have an hour glass figure.

B: Then. you really have to exercise consistently and regularly. I will go for a run. I run about half an hour everyday. Would you like to join?

A: Definitely.

B: I'm sure that you'll lose some weight in one month.

I do situps fifty times a day.

I do stretching at least 5 minutes a day.

I do jump rope.

I do aerobics.

I do pilates.

I can ski.

I enjoy snow boarding.

I enjoy wind surfing.

I like to play basketball with my friends.

Conseco Field House in Indianapolis, Indiana. Indiana team (Pacers) plays basketball with the other team.

Situation 2:

A: Do you take P.E. classes? (Physical education)

B: Sure. P.E class is one of the elective subjects.

I like to exercise using an elliptical trainer.

I use treadmill around 30 minutes for cardio-vascular exercise.

I need to do cardio everyday.

Cardio exercise is swimming, biking or running.

I like to dance. I enjoy line dancing.[1)]

I want to learn ballroom dancing.[2)]

Ball State University gymnasium (Muncie, India), I used to go to this gym to swim or to workout.

---

1) line dancing
2) ball room dancing 무도회에서 추는 춤. ball 무도회

Reading

Conner says that most people can walk throughout life. Please try the following walking activities daily. Conner (2004) suggested the following ideas.

1) Park on the opposite side of the mall from your destination.
2) Walk every aisle in the grocery store, even if you don't need anything in some aisles.
3) At work, deliver things personally, instead of using interoffice mail.
4) Go for a five-minute walk around the block when other people take their smoking break.
5) Hide your television remote control so that you have to walk to change channels between shows.
6) Play catch or hide-and-seek with your kids.
7) Spend time with a toddler.
8) Get up from your desk and take a three-minute walk around the hall every hour.
9) Get up and walk between meal courses.
10) Go to the bathroom on a different floor than you're on.

(Conner, pp.72-73)

Exercise:

1. Please share your exercise routines with your partner.

2. What do you have to do to develop your muscles? Show your muscles to your partner. Do you have six packs?

3. How many times do you workout at the gym regular basis?

4. If you do not have time to exercise, what options can you think of?

5. Write five examples of exercise.

Please write the following sentences in Korean.

1. 아이들과 숨바꼭질 놀이를 해라.

2. 나는 유산소 운동을 하기 위해서 러닝머신을 30분 사용한다.

3. 당신은 규칙적으로 운동을 합니까?

4. 나는 하루에 30분씩 달리기를 합니다.

5. 나는 하루에 50번씩 윗몸 일으키기를 합니다.

Activity:

How would you like to propose to your boy (girl) friend in the future? Let's play this romantic activity with your partner. You have to fill in the blanks before do this activity.

	The proposal: young man		The proposal: young woman
1	My little (dessert) ____________, have I ever told you how much I love you?	2	Yes, my little (animal) ____________. I love you too.
3	I have a very (adjective) ____________ question to ask you.	4	Oh? What is it?
5	Will you...? Will you?	6	Come on. What is it my little (fruit) ____________?
7	(Taste adjective) ____________ heart, you know, we've been dating for (number) years now.	8	Really, I thought it was (number) ____________ years.
9	Do you remember our first date?	10	I'll never forget. We went to the (public place) ____________.
11	Didn't we (sports verb) ____________ all evening?	12	Yes, and after that didn't we (party verb) ____________ till morning?
13	Yes. That's when I fell in love with you.	14	And do you remember when we went to (faraway place) ____________?
15	Yes, we had that (adjective) ____________ (natural disaster) ____________.	16	I remember. That was the first time you touched my (part of the body) ____________.
17	That's right. Oh, darling, will you....?	18	I don't have all day. What is it?
19	Will you marry me?	20	(Expression of anger) ____________!?
21	What?	22	Just kidding. Of course, you silly little (vegetable) ____________. I'll marry you.
23	You will? Oh, I'm so (emotion adjective) ____________.	24	Me too.

Ready-made English. North Star Publishing Company. 1995.

Learn English through Music and Lyrics

Somewhere, over the rainbow, way up high,
There's a land that I heard of once in a lullaby.
Somewhere, over the rainbow, skies are blue,
And the dreams that you dare to dream really do come true.

Someday I'll wish upon a star
And wake up where the clouds are far behind me.
Where troubles melt like lemon drops,
Away above the chimney tops,
That's where you'll find me.
Somewhere, over the rainbow, bluebirds fly.
Birds fly over the rainbow,
Why then - oh, why can't I?

If happy little bluebird fly
Beyond the rainbow
Why, oh, why can't I?

Exercise:

Please answer the following questions.

1. What is the title of this song?
2. Have you seen the movie *Wizard of OZ*?
3. Let's learn some famous lines from this movie.

   "There is no place like home."

   "Toto, we're not in Kansas anymore!"

   "Just follow the yellow brick road."

4. How can you make your dreams come true?
5. How would you wish upon a star?
6. Is there any place where troubles melt like lemon drops?
7. What kinds of dreams would like to achieve?
8. Who are the main characters of the *Wizard of Oz*?
9. If you saw bluebirds fly in the sky, how would you feel?
10. If you saw the rainbow, how would you feel?

Let's study the following expressions.

1. dare to.....

   I dare to dream

2. Dreams really do come true.

Listen to the song and fill in the blanks. (Cloze test)

Somewhere, over the rainbow, way up high,
There's a land that I heard of once in a __________.
Somewhere, over the rainbow, skies are _______,
And the dreams that you dare to dream really do ________ ________.

Someday I'll wish upon a ______
And wake up where the _______ are far behind me.
Where ________ melt like lemon drops,
Away above the _______ tops,
That's where you'll find me.

Somewhere, over the rainbow, bluebirds _____.
Birds fly over the rainbow,
Why then - oh, why can't I?

If happy ______ bluebird fly
______ the rainbow
Why, oh, why can't I?

07 Unit

Spring is around the corner.

Ice breaking activity:

1. Let's play scissors, paper, rock!
2. Look at those pictures and try to describe three positive things. You will learn how to see things positively.
3. Let's play hide-and seek. I'm it.

1. Spring is around the corner. Spring is my favorite season. There are many beautiful flowers in the spring. Let' study the names of flowers.

What kind of flowers do you like?

I like baby's breath.

I like roses.

Daffodils are my favorite flowers.

In spring, we can enjoy beautiful flowers such as golden bells, magnolia, azaleas, daffodils, and cherry blossoms.

2. Gunsan is famous for its beautiful cherry blossoms. Cherry blossom beauty pageant is held every spring in Gunsan. One of my friends was the first runner-up at a beauty pageant.

However, every spring, we should be careful about yellow dust phenomenon. How can we prevent ourselves from yellow dust? Well, we need to wash our hands thoroughly several times a day. (foot and mouth disease, bird flu, swine flu)

3. Morning glories are beautiful. The hedge is covered with morning glories. I saw beautiful hedges in the residential area in Vancouver, Canada. It was very impressive.

4.

A: What kinds of fruits can we eat in spring?

B: I love to eat strawberries (blueberries, tangerines) in spring. I try to eat one apple a day. "One apple a day keeps doctors away."

A: What kinds of vegetables do you like to eat in spring?

B: Cherry tomatoes, broccoli, cucumber, carrots, bell peppers, potatoes, sweet potatoes and so on.

5. Every spring, I like to recite a beautiful poem "My heart leaps up" by the British romantic poet William Wordsworth.

"My heart leaps up when I behold
A rainbow in the sky:
So was it when my life began;
So is it now I am a man;
So be it when I shall grow old,
Or let me die!
The Child is father of the Man;
And I could wish my days to be
Bound each to each by natural piety."

6. There is another poem by T.S. Eliot "The Waste Land." This is called as the one of the most important poems in the 20th century.

"April is the cruelest month, breeding
Lilacs out of the dead land, mixing
Memory and desire, stirring
Dull roots with spring rain.
Winter kept us warm, covering
Earth in forgetful snow, feeding
A little life with dried tubes."

I. Write the following expressions in English.

1. 어린이는 어른의 아버지이다.

2. 하늘에 있는 무지개를 볼 때 내 마음이 뛴다.

3. 나는 매일 매일이 자연에 대한 경허함으로 이어지기를 바란다.

4. 4월은 잔인한 달이다.

5. 겨울은 우리를 따뜻하게 해주었다.

II. Write the following expressions in English.

1. 나무로 된 울타리
2. 개나리
3. 수선화
4. 은행나무
5. 내 친구는 미인대회에서 2등을 했다.

We have happy to have four seasons in Korea. In each season, we can plan something exciting and special.

Summer

Summer is the season of roses. Roses are beautiful, but they have sharp thorns. Summer in Korea is hot and humid. Because of the high humidity, it's uncomfortable to work outside. It's important to put on sunscreens or sun block cream (SPF: Sun Protection Factor) to protect your skin. Wearing sun block cream will prevent from skin cancer. The ultraviolet rays are strong in summer. However, because of the strong sun, we can expect good harvest in autumn.

We experience monsoon season in summer. Especially in July, torrential rainfall causes a lot of problems in Korea. It rains hard like cats and dogs for several weeks. Because of flood and mud slide, some people are killed. We need to be prepared for this kind of natural disaster. "The worst rains in over 100 years hit the capital and surrounding areas on July 26 and 27, 2011, triggering several landslides, traffic chaos, power outages and flooded roads. At least 30 people have been killed or reported missing, with a landslide in Chuncheon sweeping away a pension and claiming 13 lives, the National Emergency Management Agency said. In a separate landslide around Mount Umyeon in Southern Seoul, dozens of houses were buried under mud, claiming the lives of at least 10 people." (EBS Morning Special, July 28, 2011)

When there' no rain, we can also experience drought. After the monsoon season is over, it becomes a season of heat and mosquitos. We cannot sleep well because of tropical night phenomenon during the summer.

Typhoon can also hit the peninsula. Fortunately, we don't have tornadoes. (Summer fruits: watermelons, melons, grapes)

Autumn (fall)

We can find some ginkgo trees and maples in our campus. Autumn is the season of harvest. During the fall, colored leaves and fallen leaves are beautiful. People enjoy wearing trench coats in the fall.

(Fall fruits: pears, persimmons, dried persimmons, chestnuts)

Winter

Winter in Korea is wet cold. On the other hand, Mongolia has a long winter but it's dry cold. People sometimes have a serious attack of frostbite of their toes. It's good to wear layers to keep yourself warm. Wearing undergarments or long johns helps you to stay warm. (Winter fruits: peanuts, walnuts)

Write the following expressions in English.

1. 한국의 여름은 덥고 습도가 높다.

2. 피부를 보호하기 위해 선크림을 바르는 것이 중요하다.

3. 여름에는 적외선이 강하다.

4. 가을은 수확의 계절이다.

5. 겨울에는 동상에 걸릴 수 있다.

Writing Exercise:

1. Please write some examples of natural disasters in the world.

2. What did you learn about the tsunami which was happened in Japan in 2011?

3. What were the main reasons of landslide which was happened in July 2011 in Seoul?

4. What are the results of torrential rainfall?

5. Please share your ideas to prevent natural disasters.

Can you follow instructions?[1)]

The following test is to see how well you can follow instructions. But you have only 5 minutes in which to complete it so you will have to work quickly. Have a pen or pencil ready and begin when your teacher says Start. You must stop immediately when your teacher says "Time's up!" You must not talk to anyone else in the class or let them see your paper. Good luck!

1. Read through the questions carefully first.
2. Write your surname in the left-hand box above.
3. Draw a circle around the word surname in sentence two.
4. Draw two small triangles in the right-hand box above.
5. Put an "X" inside each triangle.
6. Put a circle around each triangle.
7. Write your first name in the middle box above.
8. Write Yes, I can after the title.
9. Put a circle around the word follow in the title.
10. Underline sentence 5.
11. Multiply 123 by 76 and write your answer in the following box: [ ]
12. Underline the seventh word in sentence 4.
13. When you reach this sentence, stand up, clap your hands twice then sit down again.

1) Watcyn-Jones, P. Grammar: *Games and Activities for Teachers.* 1995. Penguin Books. p.110.

14. Write your teacher's name in this box. ☐
15. Cross out the second word in the sentence which begins with the word Read.
16. Draw a tree in the box in the bottom right-hand corner of the page.
17. Draw a picture of the sun above the tree you have just drawn.
18. When you reach this sentence, say out loud I have reached sentence eighteen!
19. Count up all the words in the first three sentences. Write the total in the following circle. ◯
20. Put a circle around every the in the first ten sentences.
21. Find the word carefully in one of the sentences and underline it.
22. When you reach this sentence, walk to the door, touch it and say, I have almost finished.
23. Cross out the odd numbers in front of each sentence.
24. Now that you have read through all the sentences, just write your name here.____________

Miming activity: Pair work

Car ride

1. You're going to take a ride in your car.
2. Take out your car key.
3. Unlock the car door.
4. Open it.
5. Get in.
6. Start the engine.
7. Fasten your seatbelt.
8. Release the hand brake.
9. Put the car in the first gear.
10. Drive away.
11. Change to second gear.
12. Speed up.
13. Shift into third.
14. Uh-oh! Too fast! Here comes a policeman.
15. Pull over to the side of the street and stop.
16. Roll down the window.
17. Say, "I'm sorry, officer."
18. Start to cry.
19. That did it!
20. He's not going to give you a ticket this time.

Useful expressions

ⓐ police officer
ⓑ traffic lights
ⓒ zebra crossing
ⓓ pedestrian crossing
ⓔ bus only lane

Months and events

January: New Year's Day (Lunar New Year)
Happy New Year!

February: Valentine's Day
Happy Valentine!

March: March 1st Movement
Happy Easter

April: April Fool's Day, Arbor Day (tree planting day)
"April showers bring May flowers."

May: Children's Day (May 5)
Buddha's Birthday
Labor Day
Parents' Day (Mother's Day, Father's Day)
May is the month of appreciation.
June: Memorial Day (June 6)

July: Constitution Day (July 17)

August: Independence Day (August 15)

September: Korean Thanksgiving holidays

October : Korea Foundation Day (October 3)

November:
December: Christmas
Christmas shopping
Year end party

Spring at Howon University is crowded with vibrant freshmen and beautiful flowers. Spring is my favorite season. We can see beautiful golden bells, azaleas, magnolia trees, daffodils and other flowers. What are your favorite flowers in spring?
(Picture from Howon Gallery: www.howon.ac.kr)

08

Unit

Let's have some brunch!

Situation 1:

A: Let's have some brunch this weekend.
Can you recommend a good restaurant?

B: Where would you like to go?

A: I like pancakes with maple syrup for my brunch.

B: Well, McDonald is a good place for brunch on Saturdays. They serve good brunch with coffee. It's reasonable price. There are some inexpensive brunch restaurants these days.

A: That's an excellent idea. Where else can we go for brunch in the neighborhood?

B: How about Paris Baguette? It's one of the popular bakeries in our neighborhood. They also serve brunch. Especially we can order eggs with croissant sandwiches.

A: I like my eggs sunny side up.

B: I like hard boiled eggs.

Situation 2:

A: Let's go to the cafeteria. (Let's grab something to eat.)

I'm hungry.

I'm starving.

I can eat a horse.

B: Lunch is on me. (It's on me.)

I'll treat you.

It's my treat.

A: Let's go dutch. (Let's split the bill.)

Situation 3:

A: Are you a vegetarian? Are you a vegan?

B: Yes. I only eat some dairy products.

Situation 4:

A: Can you recommend good food to keep in shape? I'm on a diet.

B: Chicken breast is good to keep in shape.

White meat is healthier than red meat.

Fish is good for health. Fish contains much omega three which is necessary for our health.

Situation 5:

A: What are side dishes?

B: The example of side dishes are as follows: Bean sprout soup, bean paste stew, kimchi, Korean barbecue, fried fish, tofu (bean curd), cucumber carrots, beef soup, spinaches, fish cake soup, fish ball soup, bell pepper, sweet and sour pork, beef on the leaf, seafood pancake, kimchi pancake and so on.

Porridge is also popular among Koreans. I took some Americans to the Korean traditional chicken restaurant. We ordered chicken and chicken porridge. One American asked for brown sugar for his chicken porridge. He added sugar and he enjoyed chicken porridge. That was different way of enjoying porridge.

All kitchen utensils are cleaned through an ultraviolet ray sterilizer in the school cafeteria. You have to put your tray on the conveyer belt after you finish eating. Let's try to reduce food waste when we eat.

Please write the following expressions in English.

1. 배가 너무 고프다.

2. 오늘 점심은 내가 사겠어.

3. 계산은 각자 하자.

4. 이번 주말에 브런치 먹으러 가자.

5. 나는 채식주의자이지만, 유제품은 먹는다.

Let's study about acronyms!

RSVP: respond please, Have you RSVP for Sam's party?
(Please reply whether you will be coming to the party.)
ASAP: As soon as possible
LOL: laugh out loud
TGIF: Thank God It's Friday.
FYI: For your information (the other person will be interested in)
PIN: Personal Identification Number
TOEFL: Test of English as a Foreign Language
TOEIC: Test of English as an International Communication
PS: Post script
MIA: Missing in action[1)]
BRB: Be right back
BYOB: Bring your own bottle[2)]

---

1) missing in action은 사라지다, 잠수 타다
2) 서양에서는 파티를 할 경우, 자신이 마시고 싶은 알코올음료를 가지고 올 수 있다. Australia에서는 식당에 갈 때 Liquor shop에서 알코올음료를 사가지고 가서, 식사를 할 수 있다.

Convenient facilities in our neighborhood

1) Public library

Whenever I have free time, I go to the library and check out books. I like to read books. Librarians are willing to help the students. We can use scanner in the library. We can also check out books and use the interlibrary loan.

These days, the public libraries in our neighborhood is convenient. Some parents take their kids to the public library. There are books available for the children. It's important for children to read books in the library.

This is the typical American library. Do you like to go to the library?
Library is the best place to study. "Thank you for not eating or drinking in this area."

ⓐ How often do you go to the library? Do you like to check out books from the library?

ⓑ Have you checked out the books through interlibrary loans?

2) Post office and bank

I have to go the post office to send a package.

How do you like to send your parcel?

I like to send it by special delivery.

I have to go to the bank and withdraw some money.

I have to deposit some money.

Where is the ATM (automatic teller machine)?

I have to update my bankbook.[1)]

I have a debit card.[2)]

I don't have a credit card.

My sister has a credit card.

What's your PIN number? (Personal Identification Number)

I don't carry cash. I just use plastic money. Carrying a lot of cash can be dangerous.

---

1) 통장정리하다
2) debit card는 우리나라의 체크카드를 의미한다.

3) Vending machine

A: I am thirsty. I would like to drink a soda.

B: The vending machine is in the lobby. Do you have some coins?

A: No, I have only one thousand won bill.

B: The machine also accepts bills. Just insert the bill and you will receive change.

4) Cafe

This is a cafe where Americans can have light meal. At the cafe, there's no waitress or waiter to serve you. That's why customers can enjoy inexpensive meals. This cafe opens 24 hours 7 days.

Let's sing and learn English.

"Tears in Heaven (Sung by Eric Clapton)

Would you know my name if I saw you in heaven

Would it be the same if I saw you in heaven

I must be strong and carry on Cause

I know I don't belong here in heaven

Would you hold my hand if I saw you in heaven

Would you help me stand if I saw you in heaven

I'll find my way through night and day

Cause I know I just can't stay here in heaven

Time can bring you down

Time can bend your knees

Time can break your heart

Have you begged and pleaded begged and pleaded

Beyond The Door There's Peace I'm Sure

And I Know There'll Be No More Tears In Heaven

Would you know my name if I saw you in heaven

Would it be the same if I saw you in heaven

I must be strong and carry on

Cause I know I don't belong here in heaven."

Let's study grammar.

가정법 과거:

If+주어+ 동사의 과거형, 주어 + 조동사의 과거 + 동사의 원형

If you saw me in heaven, you would know my name.

If you saw me in heaven, you would hold my hand.

If you saw me in heaven, you would help me stand.

Please answer to the following questions.

ⓐ Why did Eric Clapton make this song?

ⓑ How do you feel when you listen to this song?

ⓒ Have you heard other beautiful songs by Eric Clapton?

ⓓ What does meaning of "Tears in Heaven?"

ⓔ Have you lost loved ones in your family? How did you feel?

09
Unit

Weekend activities

Situation 1:

A: Do you have any plans for this weekend? Will you go home this weekend?

B: No, I won't go home this weekend. I have a lot of things to do. I have a lot of homework to do this weekend. I have to finish English video project by next Monday. How about you? Do you have plans?

A: I'll go to Seoul.

B: Do you prefer to take KTX?

A: Yes. As you know, it is a bullet train. KTX stands for Korean Train Express.

B: I sometimes take a slow train when I have time. I also take express bus which is convenient to travel. It takes around two and half hours from Iksan to Seoul.

Situation 2:

A: I will go to Seoul this weekend. I will meet my friend and go to see movies. Are there any interesting movies we can see?

B: Let's check schedule online. What are you going to do?

A: We will eat and hang out.

B: Where will you eat? What kinds of food do you like?

A: I like Korean food.
I like Mexican food.
I like Italian food.
I like Vietnamese food.
I like American food.
I like Chinese food.

B: Korean food is hot and spicy.
Some food is greasy and high in calories.
I have to watch my weight. I'm on a diet.
I want to lose some weight.
I gained a few kilograms.
I have to lose a few kilograms.

We can enjoy delicious Chinese food at the Chinese restaurant. "Chung" is one of the luxurious Chinese restaurants in 삼청동, 서울. You have to book in advance to dine in this restaurant.

Situation 3:

A: Do you have any plans this weekend?

B: No, I do not have any plans in this weekend.

I will not go anywhere.

I will stay at the dormitory and do some laundry.

A: Do you have to pay to use the washing machine?

B: No, it's free.

You need to provide detergent.

A: How do you dry your laundry?

B: I use a dryer. I have to pay to use the dryer.

Situation 4:

A: Let's go to the bar.

B: What would you like to drink?

A: How about some beer?

B: That's a good idea.

A: Cheers! (Let's make a toast!)

B: Bottoms up!

Situation 5:

A: Call me, please when you are free.

B: What's your cellular phone number? (mobile phone)

A: It's 010-9759-4301. You can leave your voice mail in my mobile phone.

B: OK, I'll. I'll text you.

Email me, please.

Fax me, please.

Tweet me, please.

Follow me, please.

Public Transportation

In Korea, the public transportation system is excellent.

I take the subway to commute.

I take the bus. I sometimes take a taxi.

When I go to work, I take the subway and then I transfer to take a bus. It's free transfer which is so convenient. I also use commuter bus.

There are nine subway lines in Seoul.

subway line 1
subway line 2 (green line)
subway line 3 (orange line)
subway line 4 (blue line)
subway line 5
subway line 6
subway line 7
subway line 8
subway line 9

Situation 1:

A: Where's the Samsung subway station? I have to go to the COEX mall.

B: You have to take subway line number 2 and get off at Samsung station.

A: I like to hang out in the mall.
I'm going to meet my friend at COEX (Convention & Exposition Center)

B: Have a great time with your friend.

Situation 2:

A: What is a mall?

B: A mall is a narrow and long place where you can walk around and shop.

A: Let's go to the movies.

B: That's a great idea. I'll wait for you at the gate number 5. There are 17 movie theaters at COEX Mall.

A: Are there any escalators at the station? (Are there any elevators?)
I need to use a lift.

B: Of course.

During rush hour, the subway is very crowded. It is packed like sardines. There's a safety wall to protect people from falling on the tracks in the subway station. You can scan your card when you take the subway or take a bus. You don't need to use cash. You just use card. It will be deducted from your bank account automatically.

Public Transport for Physically Challenged

by Seo Eun-mi (*The Korea Times*, April 28, 2009)

Recently, I happened to take one of the new buses in Gangnam, the commercial and residential area developed relatively recently south of Han River.

The vehicle was a brand new model specially designed for those bound to wheelchairs. I was really glad to take that kind of bus even though I've never seen anyone in a wheelchair on the intra-city public bus even before. Now was I sure how many of these special buses are running around Seoul.

It's quite uncommon to run into wheelchairs users on the street. In fact, I've barely seen any on the subway or intra-city buses. Every year, many people get into accidents of various kinds and degrees, with some of them ending up confined to wheelchairs. Unfortunately, most of them experience extreme inconvenience in using public transportation, so much so that many give up leaving their homes when absolutely necessary.

How can we encourage and help them? I hope to see more buildings and public transportation facilities friendly to physically challenged people in our country.

Happily, there are signs that things are heading in this direction. For instance, over the past decade or so, there have been more elevators and escalators installed at subway stations and on buses, indicating concern on the part of our government for the special needs of some of its citizens.

A good model to build upon is the emphasis American society places on such special needs. I've heard that all buildings should accommodate special needs, especially toward those confined to wheelchairs.

I remember being surprised to see some desks specially designed and equipped to left-handers in American classrooms. On a visit to Hawaii, I saw a bus driver help a passenger in a wheelchair get aboard bus. Even though it took a few extra minutes away from the bus departure time, no one complained about taking some time for one passenger. I really admired the advanced facilities- and warm, caring minds - for the handicapped in the United States.

I must keep familiar with this matter, as I teach at a university and suffer from a slight handicap myself. As a young girl, I was stricken by polio and now suffer a slight walking disability. Although I have little difficulty moving around compared with other physically challenged people, I still experience difficulty taking the stairs in subway stations and I always have to hold the rail for support.

Unfortunately, while I can't help acknowledging advancements in our society such as the bus I rode in Seoul, Korea still doesn't have basic essentials such as elevators for the physically challenged, unlike most buildings in the United States.

Yes, it's wonderful to have more elevators at subway stations for senior citizens and the physically challenged, but there's much more that needs to be done in this important area of humanitarian compassion.

Questions:

1. Are there the physically challenged in your neighborhood?

2. What kinds of facilities do we need for the physically challenged in Korea?

3. Are you willing to help them?

4. Why can't we find the physically challenged in the street? Where are they?

5. Share your opinion about the physically challenged.

Trip to Jeju (June 2011)

Hyatt Hotel in Jeju
Jeju will be one of the most popular tourist destinations for the local Koreans. Jeju Island is called Hawaii of Korea.

Unit 10

Do you likes movies?

What kind of movies do you like? I like romance movies.
I like war films. I like thrillers. I like comedies.
I like animated films. I like action movies.

I enjoy watching movies to study English. Watching movies helps me to improve my English. I learn a lot of things through movies. I like inspirational movies such as *The King's Speech*. Colin Firth is the leading actor. He's a British actor.

The King's Speech is a 2010 British historical drama film. This film is about how King George VI overcomes his stammer. Lionel Logue who is an Australian speech therapist helps the king. The two men become friends as they work together, and after his brother Edward VIII abdicates, the new king relies on Logue to help him make a radio broadcast on the day that Britain goes to war with Germany at the beginning of World War II. It reminds me of Somerset Maugham (1874−1965) who was also a stammer. Somerset Maugham overcame his obstacles and became a great writer. He wrote *Of Human Bondage* and *The Moon and Sixpence*.

(Scene captured from *The King's Speech*, www.youtube.com.)

Colin Firth

"As George VI in *The King's Speech*, he revealed the vulnerability and sense of inadequacy that can be found even in the high and mighty. Colin's innate decency, self-discipline and self-deprecation make him in the archetypal Englishman. His kind, thoughtful, passionate soul makes him into Everyman." (*TIME* May 2, 2011)

A: Would you like to watch movies on Friday night?

B: That will be a wonderful idea.

A: What kind of movies do you want to watch?

B: I like movies which I can learn valuable lessons. I like inspirational movies such as *The King's Speech*.

Please answer to the following questions.

1. Who is your favorite actor? Why do you like him?

2. Who is your favorite actress?

3. Who's the leading actor in this movie?

4. Who's the leading actress?

5. Who's the supporting actor?

6. Who's the supporting actress?

7. Who is the director?

8. Who's the producer?

9. What kind of movie you like to watch?

10. What movie did you watch recently?

Let's study English through titles of movies and dramas.

Aviator
Beauty and the Beast
Cast Away
Cocktails
Copycat
Crime and Punishment
CSI (Crime Scene Investigation)
Dancer in the Dark
Deer Hunter
Desperate Housewives
Dark Knight
Gladiator
Gone with the Wind
Gravity
ER (Emergency Room)
Farewell to arms
For Whom the Bell Tolls
Four Funerals and Three Marriages
Grey's Anatomy
Killing Fields
Kite runner
Holocaust
Immortal Beloved
It's complicated.
Legally Blonde
Little Mermaid

Lord of the Rings
Love Affair
Love actually is all around
Mamma Mia!
Mission
Mission Impossible
My Fair Lady
Out of Africa
Passion of Christ
Pirates of Caribbean
Pride and Prejudice
Ransom
Remains of the Days
Roman Holiday
Room with a View
Saving Private Ryan
Sense and Sensibility
Sleepless in Seattle
Snow White
Ten Commandments
Terminator
The Blind Side
The Phantom of the Opera
The Social Network
You've got Mail
War and Peace

The Most Influential People in the World

1. "Aung San Suu Kyi: Burma's flame of democracy
As the leader of Burma's democracy movement and a winner of the 1991 Nobel Peace Prize, Aung San Suu Kyi, is an Asia hero and global inspiration." (*Time* 100, May 2, 2011)

"Aung San Suu Kyi is released from house arrest to a Burma that, while still in the generals' grip, is changing fast. To get things done, she will have to learn how to be more than an icon of democracy."
(*Time*, November 29, 2010, p.20)

2. Mark Zuckerberg: the founder of Facebook
"He was chosen The 2010 Person of the Year. Mark Zucherberg and Facebook are changing how we interact-and what we know about each other." Born in 1984, the same year the Macintosh computer was launched, he is both a product of his generation and an architect of it. The social networking platform he invented is closing in on 600 million users. In a single day, about a billion new pieces of content are posted on Facebook. (*Time* December 27, 2010, p.31). He was a son of dentist and he studied at Harvard University. His biographical story is reflected in the movie *The Social Network*.

3. Michelle Obama:
"Declaring herself "First Mom," Michelle Obama got right to work on the defining issues of her children's generation: Obesity and improving the health of America's kids."
Her Let's Move campaign put obesity in the headlines in part because Americans under 25, are the first generation expected to live shorter lives than their parents because of diet related illness. (*Time* 100, May 2, 2011)

I. Aung San Suu Kyi

① What is the nationality of Aung San Suu Kyi?

② What happened to her?

③ How long has she been confined in her house?

④ Why did she receive Nobel Peace Prize?

⑤ What is the political situation in Burma?

II. Mark Zuckerberg

① Who is Mark Zuckerberg?

② When was he born?

③ How did he change the social networking system?

④ Are you also using Facebook to connect with your friends?

⑤ Where did he study?

III. Michelle Obama

① What's the role of the First Lady?

② What are the one of the big issues among American children?

③ What are the good ways to prevent obesity?

④ What is the life expectancy in Korea?

⑤ Please write down your own impression about Michelle Obama.
What did you learn from Michelle Obama?

IV. Please write about your role model in your life.

Talking about celebrities

Michael Jordan

He was born in February 17, 1963. He has BA from the University of North Carolina. He is one of the great basketball players in the world. He's so humble and he tried hard to be a great basketball player. I respect him since he contributed so much to the society.

Bill Gates

He was born in October 28, 1955. He was a dropout from Harvard University. He founded the Microsoft Cooperation. He lives in Seattle. He was a kind of genius. When he was introduced to a girl at college, he used to ask a question such as "What is your SAT score?" Most girls did not like that kind of question. He got married when he was about late 30s.

Madonna

She was born in August 16, 1958. She won the Golden Globe award for her role in *Evita*. Evita was the wife of the former president Peron in Argentina. She was popular among the lower class and she was successful to lead populism. The famous song by Evita is "Don't cry for me Argentina."

Famous quotes

"To tweet or not to tweet." (*Time* April 11, 2011)

"To be or not to be. That's the question." (*Hamlet*, Shakespeare)

11
Unit

What are your vacation plans?

Ice breaking activity:

Wednesday is called a "hump day" which means close to the weekend. For me, everyday is a wonderful day. Let's make everyday special because everyday is a gift.

Marvelous Monday
Terrific Tuesday
Wonderful Wednesday
Thrilled Thursday
Fabulous Friday
Super Saturday
Splendid Sunday

Grammar:

Will: for possible plans before you've made a decision

Is going to: for plans you've decided on

A: What are you going to do for vacation?

B: I'm going to visit my relatives.

I'm going to travel around Korea.

I'm going to have a part time job.

A: How much can you get paid per hour when you have a part time job?

B: It depends on the job.

I can get paid around KRW 5,000 per hour.

I have to save some money to pay my tuition.

A: What are you going to do during vacation?

B: I will probably go camping.

I guess I'll go to Mongolia.

A: Really? That sounds like fun.

Did you make plans for your summer vacation?

Did you make plans for your winter vacation?

How long is your winter vacation?

It's around two months.

In America, they have only a couple of weeks for winter break. They begin their spring semester in the first or second week of January. After they study for eight weeks, they'll have a spring break that lasts about one week. During spring break, many students go to Florida to enjoy the beautiful weather there. It is different from the Korean school system. We don't have spring break.
In Korea, the school year begins in March. On the other hand, in American universities, the school year begins in the fourth week of August. One semester is 16 weeks.

Vacation plans

*go camping

*go hiking

*go fishing

*backpacking (backpacker)

*catching up on reading

*taking TOEIC classes

*I'm going to take TOEIC classes.

*I'm planning go camping.

I'm going to go backpacking in Australia. I enjoy backpacking. You can save money when you are backpacking. I'm a backpacker. You can meet many backpackers while you are traveling around Australia. Australia is convenient for backpackers. Backpackers stay at the hostel which one way of budget traveling. In the hostel, you can cook. In one room, you have to share with other travelers. If you don't mind privacy, it's a wonderful way of traveling.

Convertible

*I'll rent a convertible and drive around town. You need an international driver's license.

*American teenagers are waiting for their 16th birthday. It is called sweet 16 because they can get a driver's license on their 16th birthday.

SUV: Sports Utility Vehicle

RV: Recreation Vehicle

*My car is a gas guzzler. It's old so that I have to fill all the time. I want to buy a hybrid car to prevent environmental damage.

Talking about vacation plans: Traveling around the world

1) Summer is the time for traveling for college students. I prefer to travel light. I don't want to carry a lot of things when I travel overseas.
I have to make a plane reservation before I travel. I can reserve plane ticket online. I'm looking for inexpensive ticket. I can even print out boarding pass.

2) There are three kinds of seats on the aircraft: economy class, business class, and first class. I always ask for an exit seat or an emergency seat. So that I'll have extra leg room. If not, it is so hard to travel in economy class. Once I was upgraded to business class. I was pretty lucky. Flight attendants (cabin crew) are friendly. Meals are complementary.

3) I have to take a connecting flight in Chicago. Chicago can be important port of entry when you are traveling in other parts of America. It takes time to go through customs and immigration. Because there are possible illegal immigrants, customs and immigration officers tend to be strict.

4) Australia and New Zealand have the opposite season. December and January are the best time to visit two countries. Unlike Korea, there is no central heating system at home. They have only a fireplace in the living room. Family members gather together around the fireplace. Koreans sometimes cook sweet potatoes wrapped in foil in the fireplace. At night, sweet potatoes are good snack. When you sleep, it's cold because there is no heating system in the room. They just use small heater.

5) In Australia and New Zealand, the driving system is different. The driver's seat is on the right. It's not easy to drive in the different system. It takes time to be accustomed to that kind of system. I was so confused to drive in Auckland and I gave up driving since I stayed there just a month.

Please write the following expressions in English.

1) 나는 호주로 배낭여행을 갈 예정이다.

2) 배낭여행을 하면 돈을 절약할 수 있다.

3) 미국 청소년들은 16번째 생일을 기다린다.

4) 내 차는 기름이 많이 들어간다.

5) 나는 뚜껑이 없는 차를 빌려서 여행가고 싶다.

6) 나는 외국으로 여행갈 때 짐을 가볍게 가지고 간다.

7) 나는 비행기에서 출입구 쪽 좌석이나 비상구의 좌석을 원한다.

8) 나는 시카고에서 비행기를 갈아타야 한다.

9) 비행기 승무원들은 친절하다.

10) 비행기에서 식사는 무료로 제공된다.

Quotations

1. "Let my people go!" (Moses)
2. "I can resist everything except temptation." (Oscar Wilde)
3. "England is a nation of Shakespeare." (Napoleon)
4. "I have nothing to offer but blood, toil, tears and sweat." (Winston Churchill)
5. "I came, I saw, I conquered." (Julius Caesar)
6. "We are not amused." (Queen Victoria)
7. "You can fool all the people some of the time, and some of the people all the time, but you cannot fool all of the people all of the time." (Abraham Lincoln)
8. "I cannot tell a lie, I did it with my little hatchet." (George Washington)
9. "The report of my death was an exaggeration." (Mark Twain)
10. "Workers of the world, unite!"
11. "Let them eat cake." (Marie Antoinette)
12. "I think, therefore I am." (Descartes)
13. "An oral contract isn't worth the paper it's written on." (Sam Goldwyn)
14. "That's one small step for a man, one giant leap for mankind." (Neil A. Armstrong)
15. "All animals are equal, but some animals are more equal than others." (George Orwell)

(*Grammar Practice Activities*, 2007, p.138)

My experience: Lessons from Traveling

by Seo Eun-mi

I like to travel around the world whenever I have time. Luckily, because my job allows fairly long vacations, I can travel to many places. I'm an explorer who loves the experiences of visiting other countries and learning their ways and customs. As result of these trips I have some unforgettable memories I'd like to share with you.

In the summer of 2007, after a teaching assignment at Mongolia International University, I flew to Beijing to learn a little bit about our giant neighbor – China. I had never been there before, and, since I teach Chinese students at Howon University, I felt it was time to experience their country and culture for myself. I booked a hotel that was reasonable and comfortable enough to stay several days.

One day after I checked in, I received a phone call from the front desk. The hotel manager told me that she needed a twin bed badly for two male guests. She asked me if I'd be willing to move to another room. Frankly I did not want to go through the hassle of repacking my bags and moving.

But, and to my great surprise, she offered me a suite room. When I entered, I was really happy to be staying in a luxurious room by myself for the first time. In fact, that hotel room and the kindness of the manager made for a very positive experience during my stay in her country. Actually, I was surprised to observe the rapid development in China. How could the Chinese achieve remarkable development to that extent?

Last summer, I booked a flight with my United Airlines mileage points and they provided me with Singapore Airlines. I stayed in Singapore a few days, which was my third visit since 1993. From Singapore I flew to Auckland, New Zealand. I did not notice that the check-in officer changed my seat number.

To my surprise, when I boarded the plane, I found that I was upgraded to business class. I had already developed a good impression of Singapore Airlines through my previous flights with them. As expected, the flight was very comfortable. My seat was like a little cocoon in which I could extend my seat to make a bed. I was able to lie down and had a nice sleep during the more than 10-hour flight. I have been upgraded to business class on several other flights I've had. I must be a lucky person.

But, like life in general, we also experience both pleasant and unpleasant moments alike. When we happen to encounter and journey through the many unpleasant experiences life throws our way, we should not be frustrated or disappointed because through these we can learn valuable lessons.

For instance, this past January, I had to fly to Ulanbataar, Mongolia, to teach TESOL graduate school students at Mongolia International University. It was my fifth visit since 2006. I really enjoyed flying with my American colleague. She and I shared lots of effective teaching tips as well as developing plans for our teaching assignments during the three-hour flight.
When we arrived at the airport, something unexpected happened. The immigration officer told me that I had some kind of problem with my visa.

To my understanding, I didn't think I needed a visa since I had already visited the country four times in two years. Unfortunately, it wasn't like that. I could not enter the country since I did not have a proper visa.
There was no way I could get a permit to enter the country. I had to take the same flight back to Incheon but in a different seat. I blamed myself that I should have double-checked the visa requirements prior to my departure. It was a huge mistake and a serious waste of travel time and money. Luckily, it was a short three-hour flight.

After the experience, I thought to myself, what if it was a longer flight, say, more than 10 hours of flight? I had just flown to Mongolia in the morning and returned to Incheon at night without accomplishing anything. What a waste of time! In Korea, I applied for the visa and I flew again to Mongolia three days after because my students were waiting for me. I had to buy another ticket, as I had made a commitment to teach these students and was determined not to let them down.

Contrary to my pleasant experience in China, I learned a valuable lesson about traveling abroad that I'd like to share: always double-check important things, like visas, before departure. This will save you from going through the same trouble I experienced in Mongolia. I will continue to travel in the future. I am not sure what kind of experiences I will encounter on these trips, but I am sure that any kind of experience will enrich my personal development.
(May 14, 2009, *The Korea Times*)

Writing project:

Please write your traveling experience and share it with your classmates. Writing is a meaning making process and it is one of the most difficult skills in English. As a foreign language learner, it takes time to develop writing skill. Try to put your effort to be a good writer.

Unit 12

Do you enjoy singing?

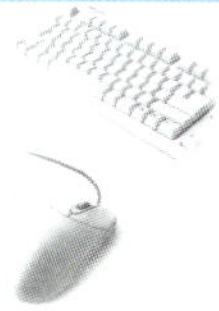

Ice breaking activity:

> We came into the world instinctively prepared to do two things. One was to suck nourishment from our mother's breasts. To accomplish this we used our sucking instinct. The other was to do everything else. To accomplish this we used our learning instinct.
>
> Peter Kline
>
> (Conner, p.195)

Koreans like to go to Karaoke room and sing with friends and family members. I cannot carry a tune. I'm a tone deaf, but I enjoy listening to music.

Justin Bieber who is a Canadian pop/R& B singer, songwriter and actor.

"Justin Bieber: The crown prince of pop"
"From the minute I met Justin, I knew this kid possessed a certain confidence that only a star could have. He was born a star. He knew what he wanted to accomplish: all he had to do was get everyone else to believe it. Now, looking back at his incredible run, the reality of who he is and what he's accomplished far exceeds anybody's expectations of him." (*TIME* May 2, 2011)

(Scene captured, www.youtube.com)

ⓐ What's Justin Bieber's nationality?
ⓑ When did he become a singer?
ⓒ When was he born?
ⓓ What are his popular songs?
ⓔ What kind of special talent does he have?

Let's sing and study English.

Aladin: Over, sideways and under
On a magic carpet ride
A whole new world
A new fantastic point of view
No one to tell us no
Or where to go
Or say we're only dreaming
Jasmine: A whole new world
A dazzling place I never knew
But now from way up here
It's crystal clear
That now I'm in a whole new world with you
Unbelievable sights
Indescribable feeling
Soaring, tumbling, free wheeling
Through an endless diamond sky
A whole new world
Aladdin: Don't you dare close your eyes
A hundred thousand things to see
Aladdin: Hold your breath - it gets better)
both: I'm like a shooting star
I've come so far
Jasmine: I can't go back to where I used to be

Aladdin: A whole new world
With new horizons to pursue
both: I'll chase them anywhere
There's time to spare
Aladdin: Let me share this whole new world with you
Jasmine: A whole new world.
Aladdin: A whole new world
A new fantastic point of view
both: No one to tell us no
Or where to go
Or say we're only dreaming
Aladdin: A whole new world
Jasmine : Every turn a surprise
With new horizons to pursue
Jasmine : Every moment
Both: I'll chase them everywhere
It's time to spare
Let me staying this whole new world with you
Jasmine: A whole new world
Aladdin: A whole new world
Jasmine: That's where we'll be
Aladdin: That's where we'll be
Jasmine: A thrilling chase
Aladdin: A wondrous place
both: For you and me

Let's learn grammar in this song.

부정사: to + 동사의 원형
부정사의 형용사적 용법: to + 동사의 원형이 앞에 있는 명사를 수식하여, 형용사의 역할을 한다.

ⓐ With no horizons to pursue, ____________________

ⓑ There's time to spare _________________

ⓒ A hundred thousand things to see ____________

ⓓ No one to tell us no _______________________

ⓔ It's time to spare _____________________________

Please answer to the following questions.

ⓐ Have you watched an animated film *Aladin*? What's your favorite animated film?

ⓑ What is the meaning of magic carpet?

ⓒ What's the name of princess?

ⓓ Who produced this film?

ⓔ Please recite the lyrics of this song with your partner. One of you will be Aladin and the other one will be Jasmine.

Vincent

Starry, starry night
Paint your palette blue and gray.
Look out on a summer's day
With eyes that know the darkness in my soul.
Shadows on the hills.
Sketch the trees and the daffodils
Catch the breeze and the winter chills
In colors on the snowy linen land.

Now I understand
What you tried to say to me,
And how you suffered for your sanity
And how you tried to set them free.
They would not listen; they did not know how.
Perhaps they'll listen now.

Starry, starry night
Flaming flowers that brightly blaze
Swirling clouds in violet haze
Reflect in Vincent's eyes of china blue.
Colors changing hue
Morning fields of amber grain,
Weathered faces lined in pain
Are soothed beneath the artist's loving hand.

Now I understand
What you tried to say to me,
And how you suffered for your sanity

And how you tried to set them free.
They would not listen
they did not know how.
Perhaps they'll listen now.

For they could not love you
But still, your love was true.
And when no hope was left inside
On that starry, starry night
You took your life as lovers often do.
But I could have told you, Vincent
This world was never meant
For one as beautiful as you.

Starry, starry night
Portraits hung in empty halls
Frameless heads on nameless walls
With eyes that watch the world and can't forget
Like the strangers that you've met
The ragged men in ragged clothes.
The silver thorn, a bloody rose
Lie crushed and broken on the virgin snow.

Now I think I know
What you tried to say to me,
And how you suffered for your sanity
And how you tried to set them free.
They would not listen; they're not listening still.
Perhaps they never will.

Please answer to the following questions.

ⓐ Where is Vincent Van Goho from?

ⓑ What are the famous paintings by Goho?

ⓒ Who's the famous friend of Goho?

ⓓ What do you think about Goho's life?

Let's study grammar in this song.

명령문: 동사의 원형을 맨 앞에 써서 명령문을 만든다.

ⓐ Paint your palette blue and gray.

ⓑ Look out on a summer's day

ⓒ Sketch the trees and the daffodils

ⓓ Catch the breeze and the winter chills

문장의 종류: 단문, 중문, 복문

단문 (simple sentence) : 주어 + 동사
중문 (compound sentence): simple sentence + 등위접속사 (and, but, or)
+ simple sentence
복문 (complex sentence): 주절 + 종속절
주절: 주어 + 동사
종속절: 접속사 + 주어 + 동사
Ex:) Now I understand what you tried to say to me,
접속사 + 주어 +동사

You took your life as lovers often do.
접속사 + 주어 +동사

Proverbs in the imperative

1. Don't cry over the spilt milk.
2. Don't put off to tomorrow what you can do today.
3. Make hay while the sun shines.
4. Do as you would be done by.
5. Don't count your chickens before they're hatched.
6. Don't cross your bridges before you come to them.
7. Save for a rainy day.
8. Never say die.
9. Don't put all your eggs in one basket.
10. When in Rome, do as the Romans do.
11. If at first you don't succeed, try again.
12. Take care of the pennies and the pounds will take care of themselves.
13. Leave well alone.
14. Live and let live.
15. Don't look a gift horse in the mouth.
16. Don't wash your dirty linen in public.
17. Look before you leap.
18. Don't make a mountain out of a molehill.
19. Cut your coat according to your cloth.
20. If the cap fits, wear it.

(*Grammar Practice Activities*, 2007, p.135)

All I ask of you from *The Phantom of the Opera*

RAOUL:
No more talk of darkness,
Forget these wide-eyed fears.
I'm here, nothing can harm you
my words will warm and calm you.

Let me be your freedom,
let daylight dry your tears.
I'm here, with you, beside you,
to guard you and to guide you . . .

CHRISTINE
Say you love me every waking moment,
turn my head with talk of summer time . . .
Say you need me with you,
now and always . . . promise me that all
you say is true -
that's all I ask of you . . .

RAOUL
Let me be your shelter,
let me be your light.
You're safe:
No-one will find you
your fears are far behind you...

CHRISTINE
All I want is freedom,
a world with no more night . . .
and you always beside me
to hold me and to hide me . . .

RAOUL
Then say you'll share with me one love, one lifetime . . .
let me lead you from your solitude . . .

Say you need me with you
here, beside you . . anywhere you go,
let me go too -
Christine, that's all I ask of you . . .

CHRISTINE
Say you'll share with me one love, one lifetime . . .
say the word and I will follow you . . .

BOTH
Share each day with me, each night, each morning . . .

CHRISTINE: Say you love me . . .
RAOUL: You know I do . . .

BOTH
Love me -
that's all I ask of you . . .

Anywhere you go, let me go too . . .
Love me -that's all I ask of you . .

I. Please write the following expressions in English.

1. 내가 여기 있잖아. 아무것도 당신을 다치게 하지 않을 거야.

2. 나의 말이 당신을 따뜻하게 해주고, 진정시킬 수 있을 거야.

3. 내가 옆에서 당신을 지켜주고, 인도해 줄게.

4. 나에게 당신이 말한 모든 것이 사실이라고 약속해 주세요.

5. 내가 당신의 안식처가 되어 줄게.

6. 내가 당신의 빛이 되어 줄게.

7. 내가 원하는 모든 것은 자유입니다.

8. 내가 당신을 고독으로부터 이끌어 내줄게.

9. 나를 사랑한다고 말해주세요.

10. 당신이 어디를 가든지 나도 가게 해 주세요.

II. Please recite the lyrics with your partner. Please pretend to be Raul and Christine. (Pair work)

13 Unit

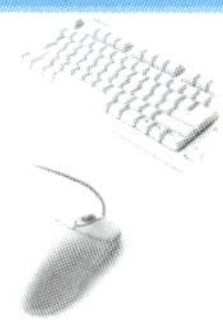

Let's throw a party!

Miming Activity:

Work with your partner. Imagine about your first date! One of you will give commands and the other one will mime.

A man getting ready to go out.

1. It's Saturday night and you're going to out with your girl friend.
2. Shave.
3. Clip your nails.
4. Take a shower.
5. Wash your hair.
6. Dry yourself.
7. Put on some cologne.
8. Get dressed.
9. Look at yourself in the mirror.
10. Comb your hair.
11. You look good.
12. Go borrow some money from your friend.
13. Buy some flowers.
14. Go pick up your girl.
15. Have a good time.

1. Where do you date?
2. Have you had a blind date?
3. What are the good ways to meet a boy friend/girl friend?

Miming Activity

It's Friday night and you're going to out with your boy friend.

1. File our nails.
2. Take a bubble bath.
3. Soak for a long time.
4. Shave your legs.
5. Get out of the tub.
6. Dry yourself.
7. Powder yourself.
8. Put on some perfume.
9. Get dressed.
10. Look at yourself in the mirror.
11. Fix your hair.
12. Put some fingernail polish on.
13. Put on your make-up.
14. Wait for him to pick you up.
15. Have a good time.

Let's throw a party!

1) Let's have a potluck party this Friday.

Let's have a pajama party (slumber party) before we graduate from high school.

What's a pajama party?

Girls spend night together to enjoy at friend's house. They just wear pajamas and spend comfortable nights.

Let's throw a surprise party for Hannah.

Let's have a Christmas party.

Let's have a baby shower for my sister.

2) Let's have a bridal shower for Minji. She's getting married next month. Are you going to be one of the bride maids?
John is going to have a bachelor party with his friend before the wedding. Samuel will be John's best man.

3) Let's have a housewarming party.
We moved to the new condominium two months ago. We're going to have a housewarming party this Saturday. You are invited to my housewarming party. (We had a ball.)

4) Next Saturday is Mrs. Kim's birthday. Let's throw a surprise party. Shall we have a potluck party? Each one will bring something to share. I'll provide drinks at my apartment.

Let's learn the following expressions at the birthday party.

* Make your wish.
* Blow out candles
* Let's have a candlelight dinner.
* You are the birthday girl today.

Marriage at Royal Family

Prince William and Kate Middleton tied the knot on April 2, 2011. Prince Harry was the best man and Kate's younger sister was the bridemaid. Kate Middleton was a commoner unlike Prince William's mother who was an aristocrat. Princess Diana was one of the most beautiful and elegant women in the world. It was a royal wedding in 30 years. It was a kind of fairy tale. They met at St. Andrews University. College campus is a good place to meet your future spouse. Who knows? You'll meet your ideal future spouse in this beautiful campus.

Conversation: Monday blues

A: You look down today.

B: I feel awful. My boyfriend and I broke up today.

A: I thought you guys were such a good couple.

(I thought you weren't going to show up.)

B: I guess we just weren't right for each other.

We don't have a chemistry between us.

A: Hopefully, that won't happen again. It'll be for the better in the long run.

Parents throw a birthday party for their children.
"Blow out your candles."
"Make your wish."

Family gathering with grandparents in one American family.
A birthday girl opens her birthday gift. (Indiana, USA)

Ice breaking activity: Whispering game:

The instructor will give you a piece of paper to the leader of the group. The group leader will try to memorize the sentences and whisper to the other member.

Proverbs in the present simple

1) A rolling stone gathers no moss.
2) Still waters run deep.
3) Eavesdroppers hear no good of themselves.
4) Love makes the world go round.
5) Actions speak louder than words.
6) Too many cooks spoil the broth.
7) A bad workman blames his tools.
8) Every cloud has a silver lining.
9) Absence makes the heart grow fonder.
10) The early bird catches the worm.
11) A new broom sweeps clean.
12) Dreams go by contraries.
13) It's an ill wind that blows nobody any good.
14) Familiarity breeds contempt.
15) Bad news travels fast.
16) The more you have the more you want.
17) Nothing succeeds like success.
18) God helps them that help themselves.
19) Practice makes perfect.
20) Two wrongs don't make a right.

(*Grammar Practice Activities*, 2007, p.263)

14

Unit

Learning English through advertisements

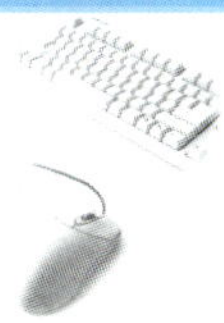

Ice breaking activity:

"Ultimately, all motivation is self-motivation. You may be offered attractive incentives, but, at best, they will only help you to decide to motivate yourself. No matter what external incentives and inducements are held out to you, you are the only person who can motivate you. This is because motivation springs from within."

Peter Honey

(Conner, p.7)

Singapore Restaurant advertisement

Dine by the Waterfront

Dine in style at Cafe Brio's where one can indulge in scrumptious dishes while lapping up the serene view of the Singapore River.

For buffet lovers, the centre island in the cafe features an exciting spread, most delicate and exquisite. There's fresh shellfish bar, salads, assorted appetizers, continental cheeses, hot Asian and western dishes and an amazing selection of deserts. "And a la carte menu is available too."

For reservation, please call (65) 6233 1100

Where magazine Where Singapore Publishing Pte. Ltd. July 2008 p.5

Please answer to the following questions.

ⓐ What are the examples of scrumptious dishes?

ⓑ Where have you enjoyed buffet recently?

ⓒ What are the examples of assorted appetizers?

ⓓ What are the examples of a la carte menu?

ⓔ What did you learn in this advertisement?

Get healthy skin for life

AVEENO Daily Moisturizing Lotion is clinically proven to actually improve the health of your dry skin.

The only natural oatmeal formula recommended by dermatologists for years, AVEENO goes beyond moisturizing to actively help heal and protect skin by replenishing moisture and locking it in for a full 24 hours. Use it every day for healthy, beautiful skin that lasts.

Mind, body & spirit Fitness April 2005 Gruner + Jahr USA Publishing. (p.13).

Please answer to the following questions.

ⓐ Are you wearing moisturizing lotion every day?

ⓑ What kind of skin do you have? (healthy skin, dry skin)

ⓒ Have you had any skin problems?

ⓓ What cosmetics are you wearing?

ⓔ Do you wear toner and moisturizer?

ⓕ Share your beauty secrets with your partner.

"Luxury Dog Spas
Los Angeles
Hollywood stars often treat their coddled critters better than they do people, so it's fitting that SoCal is studded with luxurious spas meant for the four-footed set. At The Club Beverly Hills, pooches can enjoy a soak in a Jacuzzi, practice yoga, get a massage or even work out in a landscaped yard, followed by a gourmet lunch."
(*Self.com* July 2009, p.22)

Let's study the following expressions.

ⓐ jacuzzi bath

ⓑ spa

ⓒ four-footed set

ⓓ gourmet lunch

ⓔ coddled critters

Please answer to the following questions.

ⓐ Do you have pets?

ⓑ Write examples of pets.

ⓒ What do you think about house sitting job in the western countries? If you were offered house sitting job, would you accept it?

"It takes 12 muscles to smile or 3 simple ingredients."
"Just potatoes, all natural oil and a dash of salt."
(*Better Homes and Gardens*, June 2009, p.79)

"We'll give your packages the protection they deserve."
"We do more than shipping. If you have a package to ship, let The UPS Store help. From personal gifts to business-related materials, we're Certified Packing Experts, so we make sure all your packages get the individual attention they need and professional touches they deserve. And we stand behind our work with our Pack & Ship Promise. So now all your packages will be given the royal treatment."
(*Better Homes and Gardens*, June 2009, p.17)

"The purpose of education is to replace an empty mind with open one."
Malcolm Forbes
(Conner, p.77)

Korean culture

1) Korean names

Korean names consists of three syllables in most cases. We put family name at first. Family names are one syllable but some cases there are also two syllables such as 선우, 독고, 남궁. The most common family names are 김, 이, 박. Given name or first name is two syllables in most cases. We have to teach foreigners how to pronounce Korean names clearly and correctly. In my opinion, names show Korean identity.

2) How to make Kimchi

You have to marinate Korean cabbages with salt. Sock it for around one hour. When the cabbage becomes soft, you have to rinse them with clean water. Later you add other ingredients such as minced garlic, and red pepper. Sometimes, you can put in some fish sauce. Kimchi is one of the basic side dishes in Korea. Every winter around early December, housewives make Kimchi for the whole winter. They keep a lot of kimchi in a Kimchi refrigerator so that they can eat it for the whole winter. In the past, Koreans used to dig a hole and put a big pot in the ground. Then they put the Kimchi pot in the ground. It was a great way to keep Kimchi for the whole winter. People used to help each other during Kimchi making season. But these days, some housewives purchase ready made Kimchi in the supermarket. This is evidence that life has become easier for Korean housewives in modern Korean society.

3) Summer snack: 팥빙수

팥빙수 is a summer snack for Koreans. It's steamed sweet red beans with crushed ice and other fruits or ice cream. During the winter time, hot red bean porridge is really delicious.

4) Summer favorite food: Cold noodle soup

Most foreigners are not used to cold noodle soup. They have to acquire the taste of 냉면 which is very popular food during the hot summer. We Koreans like to eat cold noodle to forget about the scorching hot weather. We sometimes put some mustard and vinegar to 냉면.

5) Floor heating system

Korea has excellent floor heating system. Some Koreans wear thermal underwear in winter time.

6) Korean age and birthdays

In Korea, age is counted even when you are in your mother's womb. Korean age is different from the American age. I was one year old when I was born in December. I became two years old in January of the following year. That's how we count ages in Korea. The first birthday is important. Parents throw a first birthday party for their kids and invite family members or close friends.

The second important birthday is 60th birthday. Koreans throw a special 60th birthday party.

7) Drinking water

These days, people don't drink water from the tap. They use a water purifier. Some people boil water to make tea. They use either roasted corn tea bags or roasted barley tea bags. There are different types of tea available depending on the people's taste. It's kind of sad that we cannot drink water from the tap. Pollution makes our life difficult. We have to try harder to keep our environment clean.

8) Friendly corner grocery store

In our neighborhood, we can find friendly corner grocery stores so we don't have to drive to a big supermarket. Life in Korea is compact and convenient. Unlike in America, it's possible to survive without driving a car in Korea.

9) Cram school

Students go to the cram school to prepare for the entrance examination. After school, most Korean students attend cram school to learn more.

10) Drive through coffee shops

11) Military service in Korea

Military is the duty of Korean males. I have to serve in the military for two years. I will enlist in the military next spring. I'm going to apply for an army. I'm not sure where I'll be stationed. I'll be paid small amount of money every month. That will be just enough to buy some snacks.
My father retired as a lieutenant colonel two years ago. My uncle served as an air force since he was a member of ROTC (Reserve Officers' Training Corps). My cousin was an officer in the marine corps. As an ex-marine, he's really masculine. Marines are well trained and they're very cooperative. There's a saying that "Once marine, forever marine."
My elder brother was discharged from two year mandatory military service.
Females do not serve in the military, however some female students want to enlist as their professional career.

Those are the ranks in the military.
*private first class
*private
*sergeant

Write down the following expression in English.

1. 나의 아버지는 2년 전에 대령으로 제대하셨다.

2. 나는 봄에 군대에 입대할 것이다.

3. 군복무는 대한민국 남자들의 의무이다.

4. 나의 삼촌은 학사장교 출신으로 공군 장교였다.

5. 나의 사촌은 해병대 장교였다.

Exercise:

1) Please write a recipe about how to make kimchi.

2) Please write a recipe about how to make Korean barbecue (불고기).

3) Please write a recipe about your favorite dish.

4) If you had a plan to invite your friends for your birthday, what would you cook? Please write your plan for your birthday party.

Exercise:

1) Do you go to the coffee shop alone?

2) What is your favorite coffee shop in your neighborhood?

3) What do you think about mushrooming coffee shops or cafes in your neighborhood?

4) What kind of coffee do you enjoy?

This was my favorite cafe run by a German in UB, Mongolia.

Regarding phone and technology

1) I surf the net to find information.

2) Please scan the photograph and send it to me by email.

3) He's a compute wizard.

4) You have to double click.

5) I like to download the music in the computer.

6) Let's have a video call through skype. It's pretty cool technology.

7) I like your ring tone.

8) My cell phone died.

9) I have to recharge the batteries.

10) I have two voice mails.

11) My sister sent me text messages twice.

12) I didn't read her text message yet.

13) Please tweet me. Please follow me.

14) Can you give me wake-up call at 6AM?

15) My alarm went off at 6AM but I turned it off.

15 Unit

Let's hit the road!

Trip to Mongolia (2006, 2007, 2009, 2010)

I have visited Mongolia seven times. My first visit was January 2006. At that time, I did not have any information about Mongolia. I just read that UB is the coldest capital city in the world. I had to bundle up to make myself warm. It was not that bad because it was dry cold. Actually during the day, I could enjoy sunshine. My first experience in Mongolia was very impressive. I was surprised at my Mongolian graduate students' English proficiency. I look like a Mongolian. Mongolians and Koreans have some common things such as blue spot which is called Mongolian spot.

When I was visiting Auckland, NZ in July 2008, the Mongolian judo player won the gold medal at the Summer Olympic which was held in Beijing, China. At that time, I felt homesick to Mongolia.

Downtown in Ulan Bator, Mongolia
We can see expensive boutiques in this building. Mongolia is developing rapidly. This is the tallest building in UB, the capital city, Mongolia. Several high rising buildings are under construction.

Korean drama 대조영 was very popular in Mongolia. Korean wave is influential in Mongolia. Mongolians enjoy Korean pops and soap operas. They learn Korean language through Korean soap operas. Jewel of the Palace (대장금) was one of the popular soap operas in this rapid changing country.

Kingis Khan (Emperor), 스크바타르 Square, UB, Mongolia

Ulan Batar is full of foreigners during the summer time. This is one of the upscale posh restaurants in UB, Mongolia.

We can enjoy two different things in Mongolia. In the city, we can experience modern life and in the countryside, we can see the nature and animals like camels and horses.

This is family ger. Ger is the traditional housing in Mongolia. Ger is built in felt. Winter in Mongolia

Trip to Japan (December 2010)

Japanese people enjoy outdoor hot spring. This is the traditional style of hot spring where you can relax.

Traditional Japanese style inn

Hot spring in Japan

Temple in Japan

Can you read Chinese characters? What does it say?

Trip to Russia (July 2007)

Lake Vikal is one of the biggest lakes in the world. Russia is famous for the beautiful women. I was mesmerized by their beauty.

This man sells Russian traditional dolls at the tourist spot. What do you call Russian traditional dolls which you see in this photo?

Russian woman plays the musical instrument.

Russian woman sells produce at the market. I could find ready made Korean side dishes here. There are some Korean ethnic groups in Russia. Korean descendents do not speak Korean language but they still keep Korean food.

Trip to Malaysia (June 2007)

A female professor from Muslim country presents her topic at the conference. Muslim women cover everything except their face not to seduce other males. Seducing men is considered as a sin in the muslim countries.

A Muslim student was my moderator when I presented at the 5th Asia TEFL International Conference, Kuala Lumpur (KL), Malaysia.

Let's laugh!

Dear John

A young soldier is far away from home. One day he gets a letter from his girlfriend. The letter says:

> *Dear John,*
> *I am very sorry, but I have a new boyfriend. You have a very nice picture of me. Please send it back. I want to give it to my new boyfriend.*
>
> Maria

The soldier is mad. He asks his friends for pictures of women-aunts, sisters, girlfriends, mothers, or cousins. He puts the pictures of the women in a big box, and he sends the box to his girlfriend. In the box he also puts a letter. The letter says:

> *Dear Maria,*
> *Please take your picture. I can't remember which one you are.*
>
> John

ⓐ Where is the soldier?

ⓑ What does he get one day?

ⓒ What does the letter say?

ⓓ Is the soldier happy?

ⓔ What does he ask his friends for?

(Heyer, *Picture Stories for Beginning Communication*, p.50)

The Young Lawyer

A young man finished law school. He opened a law office, but he had no clients.

One day somebody knocked on the lawyer's door. The lawyer was very happy. He picked up the telephone and began to talk. He pretended he was talking to a client. Then he said to the man at the door. "Please come in. I'm talking to a client. I'll be with you in a minute."

Then the lawyer hung up the phone. "Thank you for waiting," he said to the man. "What can I do for you?"

"Nothing," the man said. "I'm from the telephone company. I came to connect your phone."

ⓐ What did the young lawyer study?
ⓑ What was his problem?
ⓒ What happened one day?
ⓓ What did the young lawyer say to the man at the door?
ⓔ Then what did he say to the man?

(Heyer, *Picture Stories for Beginning Communication,* pp.103–106)

Talking about part time job

A: I'm so broke. I spent too much money in this month.
I need a part time job in this summer vacation.

B: What kind of part time job would you like to have?

A: I might work at the convenience store.

B: How much can you get paid per hour?

A: I have to negotiate with my boss regarding the pay.
I might have some flexible schedule.
What about you?

B: I would like to work as a waitress at the restaurant.

A: What about working as a cashier at the grocery store?

B: Cashier can be stressful job.

A: My friend bags at the grocery store. (In case of America)
(At the grocery store, customers are advised to use reusable grocery bags.
Plastic bags are not good for the environment.)

Fill in the blanks using past continuous and past tense.

1. While I ____________________ (eat), the phone _____ (ring) twice.
2. When I ____________________ (travel) in Australia,
I ___________ (meet) many backpackers from the other countries.
3. When Todd ___________________________ (teach) in Mongolia, he ___________ (ride) a camel.
4. While Jane ____________________ (work) in Japan, she ____________ (learn) a Japanese language.
5. When Chris and Kasandra ____________ (visit) in Vancouver, they _________ (are) in their early thirties.

Present perfect continuous

A: What have you been doing lately?

B: I have been studying hard to get a job. What about you?

A: I have been working as a waitress at the restaurant. What kind of job would you like to have?

B: I want to be a civil servant. It's so competitive.
I have to study hard.

A: Good luck! I hope you will accomplish your dream.

B: Thanks for your support. Let's keep in touch.

Please write the following expressions in English.

1. 나는 파산했어.

2. 나는 공무원이 되고 싶어.

3. 우리 연락하고 지내자.

4. 이번 여름방학에 시간제로 일하려고 해.

5. 급료에 관해서 사장님과 협상하려고 해.

My sabbatical year Muncie, Indiana (September 2009 – July 2010)

I spent my sabbatical year in Muncie, Indiana, 2009–2010. I communicated several times with Deborah who was an Assistant Chairperson for Graduate and Undergraduate Programs in English before I went to America. I was a little bit worried about the transportation from the airport. However, Deborah arranged everything thing for me. Ashley, graduate student, came to the airport to pick me up. She handed me a letter by Deborah. I was really pleased to read her letter. I was able to feel Deborah's hospitality. This is her letter.

Dear Dr. Seo,
Welcome to Ball State University and to Muncie, Indiana. We are very happy that you will be joining us this year. I am sure you'll have a lot to do to settle in this weekend. Several of our students, all of whom are here from Korea, have volunteered their assistance should you need it. My family and I would also be more than happy to help you find your way around town, take you to the grocery store, and assist you in any other way. Please don't hesitate to call any of us.

Sincerely

Debbie Mix,
Assistant Chairperson for Graduate and Undergraduate Programs in English

Debbie Mix
Cheyoung Lee
Chehee Park
Bo Young Roh

Please answer to the following questions.

1. Have you ever lived by yourself in foreign countries?

2. If you spent one year in other countries, where would you like to go?

3. What'll be the advantages living in the foreign countries?

4. How would you introduce or explain about Korean history and culture to the people in other countries?

5. How would you show your hospitality to the new comer in your school or office?

Promoting friendship between American women and international women

I was invited to join The Friend to Friend Program for International women. It was a good experience to learn how to decorate my home and how to cook American cuisine. Louise volunteered to help international students. I really value her devotion. Here is the invitation.

"Make a craft or decoration for the home."
Friend to Friend: Promoting friendship between American women and international women

The Friend to Friend program for International Women will be meeting again this semester. Our program is designed to promote friendship between American women and women from other countries, as we learn about one another's cultures. You are invited to join us. We meet on Thursdays from 10:00 a.m. until 12:00 noon.

The program is free of charge. You can bring your children as we have toys for them to play with. The programs are held at the Scheidler Community Center (Scheidler Apartment Office building). If you need transportation or more information, please call me, Louise Welty, at 396-9059 (this is not long distant).

Louise was a devoted lady who was willing to help foreign students at Ball State University. Every Thursday morning, she taught how to bake bread and cookies. We also used to do home decoration projects. She is a Sunday school teacher at the baptist church.

At the first weekend in October, Ball State University celebrates Home coming day. It was my first time to enjoy American football game.

Football team of Ball State University
American football is the most popular sport in America.

Typical American family

"Everything from Korea is pretty. You are always pretty. I should go to Korea to buy beautiful things."

Lani is 28 years old and she has four kids and another one is on the way. I was amazed how she can take care of four little kids. She asked her daddy, "Can I be just a housewife?" "Yes, you can. That is the best job in the world." What a young mother she is! She is very faithful and lovely young lady. She met her husband Travis at 태권도 school. When she was 19, Travis proposed her. Since then, they have four kids. That is right. God told us that we have to multiply.

Donna is a school bus driver at Ball State University, Indiana. I used to take a school bus and chat with her when I go to school or on my way home. She became a good friend of mine. In the North America, female drivers are quite common in case of school buses or intra-city buses.

Trip to New Zealand (2005, 2006, 2008)

I visited New Zealand three times. My brother's family live in Auckland, the biggest city in New Zealand.

Gazebo in Rotorua museum, New Zealand
Gazebo is the place where people enjoy spending time outside. We can usually find this kind of gazebo in the public park.

I visited very small place called Walkworth, New Zealand. It's was a cute little town. This butchery was established in 1922. I like to see old buildings since I value tradition. In this butcher shop (butchery), people buy meat.

Electric fences are used to prevent sheep or cows going out of the fences. There are more than 4 million sheep in New Zealand. That means, one Kiwi has at least 10 sheep.

Tea room serves tea with milk and delicacy. Tourists drop by tea room to use the bathroom.

Some Kiwis enjoy drinking with their friends at the tavern. Tavern is the place people drink and make friends. (Auckland, New Zealand)
You should never drive after drinking. DUI (driving under influence) is a major cause of traffic accident.

Senior citizens are playing crickets at the Rotorua museum. (Rotorua, New Zealand)

Seoul

Metropolitan Seoul is now international city. The population is more than 10 million. About one fourth of Koreans live in Seoul. There are some expatriates living in this mega city. Foreigners are excited to live in the capital. Seoul was chosen one of the most convenient cities in the world. Seoul is a good place to enjoy authentic ethnic food in the foreign restaurants.

The foreign restaurants are as follows.

1) Mexican
2) Vietnamese: Rice noodle shop, Rice paper

3) Thai: Thai Orchard
4) Italian: Pasta, Pizza (Mad for Garlic)
5) Japanese: Raw fish, sushi
6) Chinese: sweet and sour pork
7) French
8) Indian: curry
9) Mongolia: Mongolian barbecue
10) Franchised restaurants: Outback Steakhouse. TGIFridays

Life is changing rapidly these days. The following phenomenon are happening in Korea.

1) TV dinner: You can microwave your food for three minutes and eat while you are watching TV by yourself.

2) Throw-Away Society

The futurist Alvin Toffler talked about a throw-away society.

"We develop a throw-away society mentality to match our throw-away products." (p.54)

"Instead of being linked with a single object over a relatively long span of time, we are linked for brief periods with the succession of objects that supplant it." (p.55)

3) One person household

One person households are increasing these days.

4) Single parent

5) Nuclear family

Conversation 1:

A: My ETA (Estimated Time Arrival) is 10 minutes.

B: I'll escort you. Our security is pretty strict.

A: Thanks to you, I remember to bring my company ID (photo ID) and Driver's license. Will that be enough?

B: It is more than plenty to get you through.

A: Good to hear from you and I'll see you in 5 minutes.

B: Meet me gate 5 at Yangjae Station. Stand by Newspaper kiosk (Newspaper stand)

* The platform will be crawling with commuters.
* During the bargain sale, the department stores are crawling with hungry shoppers.

Conversation 2:

A: I'm here to visit Mr. Kim.
Is he at his office?
Can I just wait for here?

B: Can I offer you something to drink?

A: What kind of tea do you have?

B: Green tea. Black tea, herbal tea
tea with milk---English style
(Just let me know.)
(I'll let you know.)

A: You are very accommodating.

B: Just basic etiquette.

A: You are the face of the company. (EBS April 6, 2011)

References

Conner, M. L. 2009. *Learn More Now: 10 Simple Steps to Learning Better, Smarter & Faster*. New Jersey: John Wiley & Sons, Inc., Hoboken.

Better Homes and Gardens, June.

EBS Radio. April 6, 2011.

Crimson Sky. July 15, 2011. Published by Seventh Air Force, Korea.

Forbes Asia, April 2011.

Games for Language Learning, Cambridge University Press, 2007.

Heyer, S. 1989. *Picture Stories for Beginning Communication.* New Jersey: Prentice Hall, Inc. p.50.

Kurt, S. (ed.). 1995. *Ready-made English*, North Star Publishing Company.

Seo Eun-mi. Public Transport for Physically Challenged. April 28, 2009. *The Korea Times*.

Seo Eun-mi. Learning from Traveling. May 14, 2009. *The Korea Times*.

Seo Eun-mi. At the Coffee Shop. May 29, 2009, *The Korea Times*.

Time (December 27, 2010). p.31.

Time (March 14, 2011).

Time, (August 1, 2011).

Time, (July 18, 2011).

Toffler, A. 1970. *Future Shock*. New York: Bantam Books.

Watcyn-Jones, P. Grammar: *Games and Activities for Teachers*. 1995. Penguin Books. p.110.

Where magazine Where Singapore Publishing Pte. Ltd. July 2008. p.5.

About the Author

Seo Eun-mi is a professor of English at Howon University in Gunsan, Korea, where she has been teaching since 1994. She received BA from Hannam University, Daejon and MA from Soongsil University, Seoul. She got her Ph.D on Language Teaching from the University of the Philippines, Quezon City, Philippines in 1991. She got her TESOL Diploma at Saint Michael's College, Vermont, USA in 1996. Her main areas of research are content based teaching and teaching English through movies. Before she came to Howon, she worked as an adjunct professor at Hannam University, Daejon University and Hanbat University.

She was a mid career Fulbright researcher at the University of Hawaii, in 1997–98. She was also a visiting scholar in the Department of English at Ball State University, Muncie, Indiana in 2009–10.

She has taught TESOL Diploma classes at Saint Michael's College, Vermont in the summer of 2000, 2001, 2002, 2004. She also has taught MA TESOL classes at the Mongolia International University, UB, Mongolia.

E-mail: emseo@howon.ac.kr

저자소개

서 은 미(Seo Eun-mi)

- **학력**

  한남대학교 영어영문학과 졸업(문학사)
  숭실대학교 대학원 영어영문학과(문학석사)
  필리핀 국립대학교(University of the Philippines) 대학원 영어교육과 졸업(영어교육학 박사)
  미국 Saint Michael's College TESOL 자격증 취득
  한국어교사 양성과정 수료(경희대학교)

- **경력**

  현 호원대학교 영어과 교수
  미국 University of Hawaii 교환교수(풀브라이트 장학금)
  미국 Ball State University 영어영문과 교환교수
  몽골국제대학교(Mongolia International University) TESOL 대학원 객원교수
  미국 Saint Michael's College(TESOL Diploma 과정) 객원교수 역임

Making the Ordinary Extraordinary

2014년 1월 5일 개정판 1쇄 인쇄
2014년 1월 10일 개정판 1쇄 발행

저 자 서 은 미
발행인 (寅製) 진 욱 상
발행처 백산출판사
서울시 성북구 정릉3동 653-40
등록 : 1974. 1. 9. 제 1-72호
전화 : 914-1621, 917-6240
FAX : 912-4438
http://www.ibaeksan.kr
editbsp@naver.com

저자와의 합의하에 인지첩부 생략

값 13,000원
ISBN 978-89-6183-507-7